DIANA

There is still something I would like to tell you ...

Dietrich von Oppeln-Bronikowski

DIANA

There is still something I would like to tell you ...

ch. falk verlag

Original English version

Cover design by Dietrich von Oppeln

Typeset by Plejaden Publishing Service, Boltersen, Germany
Printed and bound by Druckerei Sonnenschein, Hersbruck

Printed in Germany
ISBN 3-89568-045-1

5th September 1997

The moment of the accident was a great shock. At first I did not realize what had happened. Somehow I floated above the location in that tunnel, and I thought to myself, "What a strange dream!" I did not feel any pain, but I was not in my body. I looked down on the wreck of the car. It looked terrible – this was not me, not my time – this had nothing to do with me I thought.

Then I saw a man open the back door, and I saw myself lying there. I also saw Dodi lying, bending to the other side, and it looked terrible. At that moment when I saw him I knew something terrible had happened.

Then I felt myself go back into my body which felt akward and very heavy. I did not feel the pain at first but it felt as though everything was totally wrong in my body. So I went out of it again.

I saw everything very consciously: how they put me in the ambulance, how they brought me to the hospital, how they tried to reanimate – even opened up my body, tried to get this heart going – as I watched it all, I was bewildered and in shock. Also I felt compassion for these people who tried so hard, and some of them even cried. I was imbedded in this light and power, which gave me a feeling that everything, even then, was all right.

I saw this body, my body – and I knew, it was too damaged – I saw that nothing could be done. I gave my body up – and it died. They continued to work on it in desperation, and if anybody could have heard me – I would have told them that I had decided to go, that they could let go ... and finally they did. It is not their fault ... please ... it is not their fault. They did everything they could possibly do.

I did not feel the shock any more, but I felt a great longing for my children.

I could go to them immediately, and apparently they had gone to bed when I visited them. It was very similar to how it was when I have been with them – only I could not touch them, could not kiss them in the ways I knew, but I could share all my love with them.

At that moment I did not just know, but I actually realized that I was dead – and it was a shock because I thought of them and how they would feel when they knew. I talked to them and after the way Harry moved in his sleep, I even thought he might have heard. I felt so close, so close to them ...

7th September 1997

Charles. I loved him with all my heart. Early on I saw his hidden vulnerability, something he could preserve throughout or around his education. These tender thoughts, this playfulness, his humour. Maybe it was something he had inherited from Queen Mum, this tenderness of his heart. What I also saw, was the – how can I put it – philosophical genious he was. We talked a lot about how things are in the world, what the reasons are for famine, desasters, war and injustice. I admired him because of his deep thoughts, and I believe that he liked my admiration. He saw things in a wide perspective, in a wide scope of cause and effect. So I learned a lot, and I really enjoyed debating things with him.

When he was free of his role as the prince, when he was outside the Windsor family, he was wonderful, he was relaxed, but whenever we came close to an official event he became tense and somewhat distant. He lost the connection to his heart so to speak, and also the connection to me.

It is well known, that his father Philip did not like me. But there was something deeper. I was a guarantee for something in Charles that he, Philip, could not kill – I protected this beautiful and inventive child in Charles, which Philip did not want for himself, and therefore not for his son either. Philip is full of hidden rage regarding the things he can never have – and one is – true and fresh marital love. I always was freezing when I came close to him – he hated the life-force in me. I was his blunt enemy. He did not want his son have it – a wife, a woman, a body full of life and passion. No, he did not want that in his kingdom of death.

In many ways he tolerated and even supported Charles' relationship to Camilla. Not trustworthy himself, he looked upon his son's disloyalty with sympathy. I always felt Camilla was so dead, a corpse. She was a kind of nurse, always wanting to feed from Charles' wounds and depressions – a somehow perverse relationship based on the smell of death. But this smell of death was the smell of the Windsors. The perverse pleasure of the morbid lust, that it is time to die.

In many ways I came to talk of a new kingdom – but in very special ways I came to help Charles to become King of the Heart himself. It was only after some years that I realized he would never become one. This was very painful for me. He even ridiculed me when I tried to remind him of his heart. There were many painful discussions. There is a part of him which is very able to share his love and joy, but on another level he is a Windsor, selfcontrolled, and only there for the people of Britain. For the people?

I never felt he was there for the people. The Royal Family was there for itself. It was there as a representation of the old English imperialistic colonial power – this was not the wisdom of a king.

Only the Queen Mother seems to know that – the oldest representative – but somehow she was never a Windsor. She had and has love – but she stopped saying anything – only occasionally she would say something to me, smile at me or touch me – telling me without word that she understood.

Yes, I came for Charles and my children, but mainly for Charles. And that is why it was so painful for me, when I was unable to help. That is why I cut my breast with a knife – not necessarily because of the pain I had about myself, not because of my depressions – but because of Charles, you Charles, I saw you standing there – with all the warmth and the love you seemed to be capable of but could not give to others.

I know that you were deeply moved when you took my body from Paris to England. My death touched the chamber of your soul that I was not able to open during my lifetime.

And William, Wills, oh my beloved, my beloved. What shall I say. I saw you in the battle field between us both, between your father and myself. So pain-stricken in this tension, in these two worlds which were meant to come together, to blend.

Charles and I we are both represented in Willam. And it is so important that William gets teachers, people around him who understand how to support both Charles and myself in William. Then he can become what Charles and I never could become as a couple. In many ways I have been the kind of amorphous love, and Charles was the form – also as the future king. Together we could both have made a difference. Now William will make the difference when, and if, they will let him. One obstacle for this will be his father – Charles wants to become king – he wants to become a king on his own premises – separate from his mother, from Philip – and also separate from me. A tragic figure of a king, a martyr – and he is very much in love with his martyr role. In this way nobody can have much fun with him.

Camilla supports his role as a martyr, and she likes it. In her presence he can be one.

I seemed to be a martyr – but it is not my nature. My nature is fun, life and love. I like to jump and to dance – and at one point in our marriage Charles could not stand me anylonger, because I inadvertently pressed him to choose. Being with me meant that he needed to choose to let go of his martyrdom.

But he did not want to release it. He wanted to stay how he was, and therefore he wanted to draw me into the same dry desert that he inhabited and where he finally wanted to stay. He could not stand it when I laughed and giggled like a child – he also laughed as well, he also chuckled, but most time it was close to irony or sarcasm – it was not taken from the life force

– it was something out of the reservoirs of pain. It is not easy to describe, but there was still this wonder when we loved each other, and there was this streak of humour that we shared – like children, but it happended so rarely. He seemed to be afraid of this natural und integral part of himself as if he feared that this, if shown, would be killed in himself. Therefore he wanted it to die in everybody else. It is tragic.

From my point of view it was mainly his father who made it very clear to the boy that life is not really worth living, that there is only suffering and sacrifice – and, as a compensation, slimy fun, sarcasm and a cheap sense of power.

The Queen. There were times I thought I understood her and that she understood me. There were times of hope when I thought I came close to her heart, but then I saw how much she was in pain herself. Her pain had a different character. It was the pain of loosing Britain as it was. To loose contact with its glorious history. She was so in love with the greatness of Britain, with the promise, with her mission, that she suffered a great deal when she saw the sloppiness in the behaviour of her sons. Neither Charles nor his brothers seemed to have the character and the profile. There was nobody.

So I was yet another threat. I threatened the whole concept of keeping the royalty in the Windsors' hands. Her mission and her thought was that she must at all costs maintain the monarchie in order to give the people strength and a foundation. She thought it was her duty to keep the history alive to keep the nation together, to give everybody a firmness, a strength, an inner sense of home so to speak. Jealously she wanted in many ways to be the "Queen of Hearts" herself. She wanted it to be – the way she knew it to be. She saw very well, that I could be a queen and make Charles into a king with heart.

The Queen always did what she knew she must do. I admired her for her strength and her uprightness – but sometimes I felt her jealousy. She gave her children away to the Moloch of royal education, and she also wanted that for my children. In the world I have just left it is very strange: people always want others to experience the same pain and the same hardness that they went through. They think this is virtue. So the Queen wanted my children to go through the same things that she went through and also put Charles through. She did not want to experience the shock which she might have experienced if she saw, how William would develop in comparison to Charles, William who was not going through all that pain and struggle.

If I had had any say in it, I would not have sent William to Eton.

Harry is very sensitive but not the way William is. Harry goes his own way. He will. He will reach for things without asking anybody and he has made his first decision now. He will keep people breathless with all the different things that he will do. He will be a man of justice, while William is a man of the heart and grace. Harry will say things one day, that are not even written in this book yet, through this man who is writing here and is willing to listen.

I came because the world is in deep uproar, in the powers of the old battle with the powers of the light, of the new. The powers of the old will do what they can to stop the powers of the new. I was the advocate of the new, in the navel of the world, England. In many ways England is the navel, the solarplexus Chakra of the world, the bright yellow light which supports and provides the strength for the future transformation.

I only had to choose how I completed my mission. So I had the choice of putting everything into ONE shockwave, or just creating ripples in the following years. I decided to put a shockwave in motion, because the world is so close to the change – and I could not see how I could achieve as much by any other means than this. This is not the way that my physical self, Diana, wanted to choose, but the way that my soul had chosen. I completed my life in the physical body with Dodi, and I continue my life with him now. You have no idea how wonderful it is! We are together all the time. We are full of love and fun – after we had completed our work with the shock, and our work with our pysical relatives, our parents, brothers and sisters, and all those where we came from. Here, however, where we are, we can be so much more effective.

We were not supposed to meet so early – but after both our lives took the turnings they did, we decided to fulfil our dreams with each other in physical form first, and again now in spiritual form. But we ARE together. This was OUR play. It was, it is, it will be.

Of course during our physical incarnations this was not our preference, but now we both understand.

Also by these means Dodi wants to comfort his relatives, and ask them not to mourn his passing anymore. Especially not to endulge themselves in strange presumptions, such as "there was a conspiracy" or something similar. If there had been one, it would have happened to help us fulfil our mission. Please understand. There is no guilt. No one is guilty. There was no conscious conspiracy.

23rd September 1997

I could have stayed – but it would have been so much more difficult. Yes, it is true I was pregnant. I had reached this pivotal point where I could choose. I stood there with this new power on the horizon but also with this enormous danger – danger for my children, danger for our marriage with all this hassle, with all this now even more controversal publicity. There were too many powers, and too many extremes would have torn our relationship apart. They would – yes, this is true – they would not have let us live this dreamlife unharmed.

Maybe now, in the heart of the people, my mission continues.

In our tender hours Dodi and I talked at times about what they would do to us. We pondered over the difficulties, and we mused over the vulnerability of our love. With Dodi as a Moslem, and me as a Christian – living a life in love and peace? Can anybody imagine what kind of provocation this would have been – and how many forces would have tried to destroy it, disturb it, ridicule – and who would have suffered? My family, his family, the children ...

Yes, now I can see it much more clearly than I saw it before: everybody, everybody is in the midst of the forces, between power and heart. The cold ancient power to keep things as they always were, and the new strength of love and heart. My pains and my struggles, my painstricken and destroyed marriage, my attempts to be happy and the "tragedy" of my death. For many, yes, for many of you women in the world who want to follow the path of the heart, it should give you a sign – a token of understanding for yourself and your passions. I died, but you might live, you should live, you should go for life following your heart – and never give up. I did not give up – I hurt myself, sometimes I wanted to go, to leave, but I did not give up or rather, give in. It was not possible. Each time I was so close to death in total desperation, there was somebody or something which like a ray of sun was touching my heart and I went for life again.

My death in Paris was not a suicide, no, not at all. Also I was not murdered. Yes there were some people involved and by the means of their investigations they will find this out – but they served the purpose and they will discover something about themselves. They learn ... so do the Paparazzi whom I hated so much because of their tendency to violate privacy, to violate the most precious value in people – dignity. It does not matter what it is: they take the shots and then they allow those pictures to be interpreted by those who do not know anything about the situation, or about the atmosphere and the truth at the moment the pictures were taken. It is like taking a piece of a jigsaw puzzle out of one picture and putting it into another completely different picture, which is sick and full of lies and distortion.

They need to know that their camera flashes blinded Henri, and not only Henri, but also other car-drivers who were driving through that tunnel. Henri could not see anymore and could not stabilize the car which was already skidding.

25th September 1997

When I was a child I could be in a state of exultation and joy, and also in deep despair. My father often talked about me being very extreme, very emotional, but he was very emotional as well... so probably I had inherited it from him ... I had some very lonely days, and I loved these lonely days. I had visions of a life as a queen – yes, that early. I knew Charles already at that time. In my thoughts and my inner pictures I saw myself even then as a woman with many children and the possibility of helping others. I saw the pictures where I was able to help little children, to hug and kiss poor people, to be with the old and feeble. Sometimes I shed tears about the stories of children who had no parents and I was shocked and terrified by pictures of the wars, for instance, the Vietnam war with this picture of the child who had fled from the napalm bombs.

I could feel the pain and horror of these children, of the victimized people. Sometimes I could hardly sleep for days. Also my dreams were full of that horror, my compassion, and the ways in which I could help. I often thought, if I could just ... and with my girl friends I talked and we said: If we were just powerful enough, if we were those who could decide ... we would decide differently. I often thought about what I could do to help. What kind of life I would need to have to have the influence and power to be able to help.

Whenever I had been with Charles I felt that he had compassion as well. I felt that he knew about all the terrible things which happened in the world and I trusted him that he would change it when he became king. I had good reasons to believe that he would be successful. I knew he had many different even rebellious thoughts about the royals and royalty. Also he believed that a man in his position and with his opportunities should be active and try to put his finger on things which were unjust, wrong and socially harmful. Later I found out that there was a big difference between my thoughts and actions and his.

It was strange: after our wedding I felt somehow back in a childish love to him. There was nothing and nobody but him. I did not think anymore about my dreams of my childhood. I just wanted to be with him, to help him to be a better Prince of Wales, a better successor and to enjoy our love – yes romantically – like it was promised in the wedding – yes, a fairy tale. Yes, I thought and hoped the fairy tale would go on. Yes, I was that naive.

I loved him and I also thought my love would wipe out his love for Camilla. She was experienced in all those things which I did not know or did not want to perform. Even on my honey moon with Charles I made so many mistakes regarding my behaviour as the wife of the Prince of Wales – and often I thought it was o.k. for Charles because – believe me or not – so often he mocked about the protocols himself. From early on I heard him sigh and be sarcastic about the royal duties, the code of behaviour, but any time I played on his sarcasm and really went against the rules he was angry at me. It was as though he wanted to be rebellious and sarcastic, but never really dared to live it and expecially did not want ME to break the rules. In addition there was Camilla who always was his last resort to ease his pain of being between the two worlds – the world of a free and powerful man, and a stricken Prince imprisoned in his educations, in the traps and strongholds of a childhood of total loneliness and coldness where there was nobody who was with this so tender, so ingenious and so thoughtful a boy. I could not really understand this pain because I just laughed and lived without guilt when I had made a mistake. It was different for him. He could go into deep guilt and desperation – and there was Camilla with all her understanding and all her realism which I did not have.

I can see it now, but I could not see it then. I was not a psychologist, I could not understand – I did not want to understand. This shadow in our marriage that I was a somewhat inadequate woman for him and an inadequate wife was there from the beginning. In view of what I felt for him I was unable to understand how he could go to Camilla in the days before and after our wedding – and he did it several times. I could understand that he needed somebody who could ease his pain, and the guilt about the schism in his soul – a schism I did not want and could not deal with – but it was very hard for me and incredoulous that he was with her. If I could have understood, then I would have understood the difference between Charles and I, and between Camilla and I- and even could have found a way out.

I wanted to realize my dreams together with Charles, but when I became aware that he was not interested, and did not really want to do things together with me, I started to see that I must do them alone, and I felt alone.

The years – by 83 – they started to be full of loneliness. It is not easy to describe. It was a lonliness like an echo. One says something and it echoes back. It does not touch anybody and it does not touch ones own husband. He started to retreat from me. He started to hate my kisses and my touch. I felt that he had started to hate the very warmth of my body. It was as if it reminded him of a life he could not live. Maybe it reminded him of dreams he himself had as a child. I remembered the many times I had met him when I was a child. We had had so much fun together – real pure wonderful fun. Nevertheless when there was this intimate longing of a wife, I felt that he retreated. He rejected me even then. I could not understand. I gave everything. I even did things for him I never would have done for any other man. I often said to myself at that time I would do what he said and wanted, I would do what was decent in his eyes, I would hold out, I would stand beside him in the boredom of a day with all these senseless speeches and receptions with people who have everything and do nothing – I would hold out. I would be a good wife I promised. Then, however, even then it did not seem to be enough. It did not seem to be royal enough – always there was something he told me about afterwards which had been wrong. In the nights when I was so tired and so strongly desiring to fall into his arms to love him, to be comforted, to share the joys and the pains of the day – he started to talk to me about things which had gone wrong – and worse, about what was wrong with me. I knew that he ALSO suffered under the days duties. But at night ... even at that time, there was nothing else but a prolongation of the pain and lonliness and seldom enough then did we come close to each other, maybe out of exhaustion or finally out of pure bodily desire.

If I had known then what I know now I would have seen and understood more – but it was then that I looked up to him. He was 13 years older than me, he was a man who knew EVERYTHING, so I thought, that it must be always my fault if he was angry with me or if he rejected me. I was in the role of the Princess who had found her Prince, the Prince who is clever and wise, and the Princess is just the Princess, fallen in childish innocent love. This I wanted to be, this state I wanted to stay in, and he could not handle it. I became an object of pain, and guilt.

When William was born and in the years when he grew up, my lonliness became endurable. Further more – William saved my life. From the first day I felt him in my womb, I felt there was – strange to say – the one who really loves and understands me. It was an odd feeling. It was like: here inside me is the real Charles. When I tried to battle against these thoughts they became stronger, so I did not fight them anymore. This growing life in me was a promise that everything which I thought which should happen in my life could happen – fun, laughter, compassion and love. So often

I laughed with my child, and I heard him giggle and he moved so wonderfully and was so funny. We had so much fun together.

There were also these other feelings and thoughts: What will happen when he is born? How can I protect him from this world full of misuse and misunderstanding? Nevertheless I enjoyed those nine months and tried to stay with my happy thoughts and not with the thoughts of anxiety and fear. Out of all this there was, and still is, this strong bond between myself and William.

And I want to say to you, William, beloved, that I will always be with you.

Of course this time of pregnancy bettered my relationship with Charles – but mainly because of the fact, that I was more focussed on the life in my womb than on my marital love.

1st October 1997

It is hard to imagine how it was for me when they took the children from me in the divorce contract. It was like a sword going through my heart. It was then that I remembered Mary the mother of Jesus when she said there was a sword going through her heart as she was losing her son. It felt like a double sword, a double death after the death of my marriage with Charles. It was so deep, it was so terrible that I felt completely numb. I was sick time and time again. I could neither eat, nor sleep, or even cry. I stood there at the window, grabbing hold of the curtains, leaning against them, trying to imagine they were something warm and human which could hold me. It was much worse than the divorce of my parents and the loss of my mother but it felt the same. Always, I thought, why do I always need to die, why all this dying in my life and everybody seems to think I am so alive. Yes, I am and was, yes, yes, yes, when there was only a second, a minute when I could be alive, I was alive, but can you imagine, what it is like, when one dies while one is alive, and one can only show it in a sickness which is called bulimia.

You know, and I tell you women who have this "sickness", that it is only a deep, maybe even necessary, reaction of the body to show the pain of your conflict with things how they are. One throws up, this is the "death" part and then one eats, one eats and eats – and this is the "life" part. It is like waves on which one tries to sail ones life in a storm which is called passion and desire conquering the attacks of death – through people, through circumstances.

From where I can see things now, this is the big battle in the world – between life and death – real life and real death. I do not talk here about death, the death as a completion of physical life. That death is beautiful, a friend, a light, but the real death is in the world, in people, who do not know how to live anymore, who grab hold of anything that seems to be life, like power, money, positions, old positions, old ideas, gossip, sensationalism, wars, fights, destruction and exploitation.

Then there are those who want life – such as those in the so called third world, who are so much damned to death. On my trips I met so many poor and sick who were more alive than those who have everything and live in wealth. I felt so much more drawn to those so called underprivileged – and often they were a comfort to me. How often I was bored stiff and deeply in pain in this atmosphere of death which goes with the greyness of High Society. There was no life, there was only form. Lifeless form, which could neither live nor die.

My beloved England, beloved country, you will change. You cannot carry on being the same. As in another lifetime, I came to Earth at the dawning of a new time. I did not know it then, I know it now. I saw all my lifetimes, I could see, I could compare. All of us have many lifetimes – and they are like steps. With each step we try to get further with something we deep down have as a purpose, as a focus.

Englands purpose, beloved Tony Blair, you will give it new wings. You with your charisma, with your insights, with your visions and your good heart, you can make it. You are the hope of England, you are the hope of the island, the hope of Europe even and the planet Earth. In many ways there is a connection between my death and your success, and I pray for you that they let you live and act. My spirit will be with you.

Yes there are forces in the world I left which do not want change. Which do not want heart, which want to control the souls of many, which want to control love, which want to control feelings and emotions and true power. Then what is the treasure of people? The treasure of people is love, feeling and emotions. Reason always wanted to control feelings and emotions. But it could not. Many have battled against them and have started wars – because it is true life which is going to produce change in the heart, in people and in nations.

When the wall came down in Germany I cried many tears, tears of love. My crying was born of hope in the new wave, the going forward into freedom. There were many around me at that time who looked at it suspiciously and even somewhat bitterly. I could not talk about it with Charles. Like so many others, he was afraid of a Germany who would get back to its might and power. I was bewildered that the only result they could see was this. They did not see the wonder of people bringing a wall down. I felt with these people, I cried with them, I laughed with them – I felt so much how it was when a wall of separation comes down, and when people meet and they hug and they kiss. So from this time on I tried to bring even more walls down myself where ever I could. I saw the walls constructed by politics, by morals, by religions – by those who think they know what people are like. Who knows what people are like? What they need? What their visions are, their love, their imagination?

I cried when I saw the reunion of families. Is there anything more beautiful than a family? Did anybody ever think of it, feel it? What is a family? A circle of love, a protected home, a cosy pool of care? How much strength is in a family, how much wonder? Did you ever look into the eyes of a happy child? Does it take much to make a child happy? Is it not a moment of care, of love, of a word like: "Here, darling, here I am, and I will not leave you"?

What do you think, world? What was the mission and the so called message of Mother Therese? What do you think, world which knows everything? It was the message to those who were sick and poor – it was not the message, "Come! I will heal you", but rather the message: "You are not alone ... You are not alone – I am here". This was the mission of Mother Therese.

There is so much loneliness in your world. This loneliness is what produces sickness and poverty. Please understand. Everywhere I saw lonely people – in the midst of wealth and power, and in the destruction of Bosnia. Do you know how a child, how a wounded soldier, an aids stricken man, or a raped women feels when you stroke her hair and say: "You are not alone" – whilst feeling and saying it from the depths of your heart, and looking into the eyes of the other?

Well there is help, both financial, and political, – but the most important help this world needs is love. Yes, love – yes, saying: "You are not alone". To be there, to be responding, yes responsible and responding, yes to smile, to be there from human to human, to hold, to touch, to give life, real life. This is the inspiration you need everywhere, this is the soul between people. Start to give voice to your soul, start to give voice to your beautiful emotions like compassion, like care, like sympathy. Of course, give money, give of your wealth – but give even more of the wealth of your heart.

All the flowers you have put down at Althorp, Kensington, Buckingham and other places, London, Paris, elsewhere – I saw them laid down for the people I love. I saw that the soul I stood for touched you deeply. Lay down flowers for the lonely. Lay down the flowers for those who are in despair. Lay down flowers of your heart and heal the families, give the children the feeling that there is not only God in Heaven, but there is love in your heart, love and care. Bring God down to the world – God is in the heart of people.

Don't focus all your love on Diana, focus your love on that which I stood for. I understand, oh yes, I understand. The way I lived and the way I died it reminded you of the pain and the longing in your heart.

And you women! Beloved of the world! Do you understand? You are the hope of the world – those who are in the midst of storms, of sadness, and lonliness. Start to let yourselves flow through the prisons of reason, through the walls of separation, and barbed wire territory. Take the landmines away which are laid in your fields of dreams. Many of you know what I mean.

You cried your hot tears. Beloved, take heart and be the women of the world, who talk and do what they know is right. Stay in the hope, love your families, be with your husbands, partners and understand – but do not compromise. Do not compromise with the control, or with the coldness. Because those who are cold need the warmth the most. Yes, it is heartbreaking, to see, that those, who need the love the most, are battling it so viciously.

I talked with the women in Bosnia, such strong women, and so desperate. They could not understand how God, Mary could allow all this pain. All the families destroyed, children with no parents, parents separated – not by coldness of heart but by the war. Families who wanted to stay together. So I tell you, liberate God, the Goddess in your heart. Yes, there is a Goddess – this light which is in me and around me is not male, nor female. God is both, and it is the purest love and the purest compassion, the purest joy and the purest life, you can imagine. Yes, there is life here as well – it is different, but it is life. For the first time I understand that there is life everywhere. Death is only in the minds and hearts of people.

Landmines. Vicious and so insidious, so dreadful and mean – there are no words to describe the maliciousness of that kind of weapon. One walks happily along in the sun, the birds are singing, the sky is blue and one feels peaceful when suddenly, without even noticing anything – one is crippled for life. Nothing can be done, one cannot fight it, one cannot solve or resolve anything – one just stumbles upon it and dies or is seriously wounded, literally torn into pieces. I saw children, severely wounded, in terrible physical pain and agony. I talked to many of them, but far more horrific than the wounds and the hurts were the looks in their eyes. I cannot forget. The eyes who looked at me and asked: Why?

Why? What could I say. I held a hand, I kissed a forehead, I gave a flower, I hugged, I smiled between my tears – but what could I say? How could I respond to this deeply felt:Why? of their hearts and souls. You know what I saw in the look of these children. The total loss of any trust, trust in people, in the world, in any future, in anything, in themselves. Psychiatry will not do it. Psychiatric help is definitely necessary, but what is really more important is that these vicious things disappear – and I do not talk only about the physical landmines, which are laid out in many millions throughout the world – especially against children. I also talk about the landmines in the hearts of people who allow these landmines. How dead must people be, who dig a hole and put this kind of death in it, and cover it up with earth. What has the Earth done to us, that we use her dust to cover up our most terrible and mean acts? Will she not tremble, will she not flood with tears?

The landmines in the hearts of people. One walks in love and in innocence --- when boom!! Something explodes, something one did not see or even think of beforehand, as nothing posing any threat was visible. It was put there long ago and it waited to explode.

Who puts the landmines in the hearts of people? How can one be so dead, so numb, so unfeeling – that one does this or allows it? Why do nations want to keep these amunitions alive? Amunition which kills their own children? What kind of nations are these? Do not all nations have people, families, men, women and children who want to live in peace? How can democracies in the world even try to hinder the prohibition of these weapons?

I am glad that there is somehow a stop on landmines worldwide – at least it seems that way. Not everyone wants the stop. Why? Because there are landmines in the hearts.

Dodi and I often talked and, yes, still talk about these things. He, in his tenderheartedness, understood what I was saying. He suffered under the fundamentalism of his religion. He suffered because of the cruelties in the name of his god. For him God was love and justice, and not the excuse, to kill and hurt. We often talked about what would happen when we were married. How would people understand a Christian Moslem marriage. Would they understand at all? Would it bring peace or an avalanche of misunderstandings and dissension, maybe new uproar and terror?

Between Dodi and I there was never any discord about this – when we loved each other we felt that we were held by the same God. We did not even talk about it. There was no difference. I could let him be himself, and he could allow me to be me. In our intimacy there was only love. There was no difference what so ever.

The difference is just words. We met naked, stripped of all prejudices, of all premises, and of all cultural differences. We were just man and woman – beyond any reason or judgement. This is the value of being intimate. There was God and there was us. There was our love, and there was our baby.

Yes, it is true, I was pregnant. A soul wanted to come into our life – and for me it was the most beautiful thing that could happen. I desired a child from Dodi with all my heart. A child I could keep – a child in a family which would really stay and live together. This was more important for me than to be Diana the Queen. I just wanted to be a loving woman and have a family. Nothing else mattered. I found this to be provided by Dodi and his family.

Mohamed his father. Yes, many say he is a cold-blooded businessman and all that – but I felt so protected and content in the hidden warmth of his heart. Yes he is a patriarch, but in a good way. He might be harsh – but you know: it is better to be harsh and clear on the outside whilst being tender and vulnerable on the inside. Mohamed loved me like a daughter. There was nothing I believed I could not talk about. In addition there was this love between father and son – it was so clear, and direct, based on dignity. No, not without problems, no, this is not what I am saying – but there was heart and the willingness to be honest and truthful.

Yes, I wanted this child, and Dodi was very happy. It is true that he was not without his concerns, but he was happy. We still had no name for it. No.

I dreamt these dreams of a family with Dodi, in a protected place – maybe Italy, at least near the ocean at a Mediteranian place. I saw them all there: William, Harry visiting, playing with their stepbrother, and all in the good energy and atmosphere of the al-Fayed Family. In many ways I also wanted to build this new family for William and Harry. A kind of "test" was the time with them in Italy and France. It was very peaceful, very wonderful. They liked Dodi and Dodi liked them. Especially William seemed to understand. He is so remarkably capable of a deep understanding, and so was Harry in his way.

Also I do not love William more than Harry, they are just different. Harry is wonderful in his playfulness and in his creativity. Yes, I love them both deeply and my spirit will stay with them. So I wanted them to have a real family as well since there was not one in England anymore.

Charles. I love you. I still love you from the depth of my heart. My love for you is eternal. My love for Dodi is a different one. It is possible here to love deeply and to love many with the same depth. This is not so easy in the world, but when I was still in the world, even when being with lovers and with Dodi, I never ceased to love you, Charles. You have something – and I described it in other words "earlier" – which you fight the most: Love and compassion. You are a king. Yes, you are, and there was nobody with so much understanding of the base of your being than I had. There was this ingenious child, which is now spread in William and Harry. How much I tried to awaken this child in you, this tender heart. Now I succeeded with William and Harry, who I put under the protection of the Almighty.

And you, Charles – I was so close to you when you brought me from Paris to London. I felt your heart. If I had been able to I would have written you a letter, telephoned you, and talked into your heart – but because this was not possible I am telling you through this book which I hope will reach you. Nonetheless something in you heard me. You heard my voice. And your heart was there – so strongly that you did not obey the rules and regulations anymore, and you expressed yourself the way you did in the times around my funeral. Thank you so much for being the way you were with William and Harry and still are, for the way you comforted them, the way you have been a father. It was very good and again: Thank you.

And you, Camilla, I know you think differently about me now. What happened between us often happens in the world. There are two women who could be friends but are separate and hostile because of a man. How I tried to understand, how I tried to understand the love between you and Charles.

Somehow I saw that there was a woman for each aspect of him – which talks about how torn he was between these worlds, your world and mine. Why couldn't we talk about it? To see and realize that he had chosen – and to speak about the way he is because we both loved him. What a tragedy that we women do not talk, that we quarrel about men and loose sight of each other, and all of our compassion ...

Like many men, Charles wanted a way out .. a door which he could slip through into a place where he was at peace with himself. I did not understand that then, but I do understand it now. You were the peace for his heart and mind. A peace he could not find with me, because I confronted him with the way I loved him, and it was a love without compromise. This was not because I wanted to hurt him or make him uneasy, but because I couldn't do and be differently. It was like my bulimia. When I did not like something, my body showed it – even when I tried to hide it. How often have I cried and tried to cover up – but my body showed it. How often I cried not only because if you, Charles, but also FOR you ... and I tried to hide it behind my smile or my sunglasses or both.

I am not able to cover up landmines. I never was. I never will be.

I often wondered: how can other people do this? How can they smile when they feel hurt. What sense does it make to cover up behind rules, regulations, and laws, bare behaviour? Is it not like lying? Nobody can know what you think and feel? And where will it then show up? Will it not show up in something else?

Did not my death uncover the hearts of millions, and even the heart of Charles? I am far off boasting, but look and see ...! Look and see what is the real, REAL desire of people!! Is it their desire to hide behind etiquettes and protocols? Is it their desire to protect the monarchy and their rules? Is it their desire just to behave, to cover up? What did you see in the days after my death? If this much love is in people how much more is there in their hearts? What a strength of desire and emotions...!

You saw it Charles, and I am so thankful. If this was the only „reward“ for my life and death, that you Charles are more open, more accessible for the people, your people, that you show more of what I know what you are – it would all be worth it. The way you approached people in the days following my death, how much you stood for what you believe and the way you stood for our love. I was rejoicing, and many with me ...

I do not believe it would be good for William to become king right away. If you can be, what you have shown, then you should be king and then, when the time is ripe, William should. Not, however, because it is necessary, but because then the kingdom of the heart, the spirit of England can live as a role model for the world, as an image and a path for the times to come.

There is no point in continueing to mourn. I am having too much fun and laughter, too much joy, even more here than on Earth. Please get the guilt and the heaviness out of the way. Nobody is guilty of my death, not even of the "tragedy" of my life. My life was not tragic and I am not a tragic figure as some papers have written. I always looked for the life and light, and always will ... there is always light, and life is eternal. It does not matter what names, what circumstances, what kinds of reasons and reasonings. Life just is. Either you decide you want to be life and light, or you decide to fight the life and the light you are. I hope my death showed all of you that even death only contributes to life.

I do not know where I will go from here. I will definitely come back, but for a while I will stay and help and support – from here. Yes, this is possible too and many do. There is much support from the realms from where I see and experience things now. I learn, I evaluate, and re-evaluate my existence and my existences, as everybody does who comes here. It is not hidden or mysterious. When one is here one knows it all and one understands. You all are much closer to me, than you think and I am much closer to you – I walk with you, I dance with you, I sing with you, I smile with you. At times I even cry with you, but not out of pain but of love. How wonderful are tears of love! They sweep and spill the pains away.

I experience the longing of all of you, yes, of all mankind, to reach a way of existence which is full of laughter and satisfaction, beauty and dominion – it is in everybody. So stop fighting this longing, go for it, have visions and dreams, have desires and imagination – manifest the world you desire. A world without tears of despair, a world without famine, a world which is full of the awe of the mysteries of life. Indeed, there is mystery of life, a jubilant mystery, a jubilant reality and exitement, an ecstasy ... Allow yourselves this ecstasy and bring the light into the darkness, bring light to those who mourn in darkness. Mother Therese and I work hand in hand.

So, do not mourn too long. Go with the joy which transcends darkness, which transcends pain. Care for those who do not seem to have hope, and those who are alone. Lead their souls out of the valley of death into the green hills of light and life – like the green hills of England I love so much.

Oh, Elton, oh Elton, beloved. Yes, the green hills you knew I love so much. What a beautiful song for our friends as well. You touch hearts. Go on touching them. Take the seal off your mouth and sing even more. Sing even more about the candles and the torches. Bring light through your music. So many like you stand up and bring music to the world with the messages she needs and at the same time feeding millions with the money which is coming together from these concerts. How proud I am of all of you. You, the true ambassadors of the heart – singer, musicians, artists and poets – there is no politician, no government who ever could move what you can move. Take heart. Let the emotions spill throughout the world, heal the world – yes, you as well, Michael. Give space to your passion of music – if they cannot do it, you can. Heal hearts with the values of love and integrity. Be passionate with the new visions of an Earth which can and will heal herself.

When you are here, you see things differently than you do on Earth. From here you evaluate everything under the premise: "What did I do, what was my motive?"

You cannot imagine how far one little act of love, just a smile, a touch, or a word of compassion can go. It does not matter, if it reaches millions ore a single child. Just do it, and it lightens everything throughout the world. It is as though everything is connected. What you do in London, helps in Hong Kong. If you heal a soul in Paris, one is healed in Bosnia. Yes, it is important to help with money, huge amounts of money, yes, but do not forget to feed souls too, with your good thoughts, with your good intentions, with your love for the people you love, and even for those you have difficulty loving.

From here I do not hold, and cannot hold anything against anybody. Death is a great healer, but also a great forgiver. For you see, how everything ties in with everything – and how perfect everything is.

Do not put things on Henri Paul. He is not the guilty one. Henri needs our compassion, and do not torture Trevor! Let him forget. Please let him forget. How could it be of any use now to find out who caused my death? What could it change, and how could it do any good? Can you see the beauty of my death?

If I told you that Henri wanted to go too? Would it help you to see things differently? And if I were to tell you, that Trevor decided to come back in order to fulfil a specific mission in his life, would you believe me and let him go in peace?

Why are you always so eager to find out? I am telling you: you cannot find out the reality of my life, nor the reality of my death. If you could, you would be me. Those who did not know what to say or what to do – but just were a little more friendly to others, and a bit more respectful or caring to a neighbour in the time of my death, those people understood more than those who want and are now going to explain, to research, and to find the guilty ones.

It is senseless and even harmful and not at all what I want.

You know, from my perspective here I can see more of what is in the people. I can see the layers of educations, false motives, and the beliefs piled up on the very soul beneath them, which aches and sighs. I can see that many try to do the best they can, but they do not know what is the best. This is why it is so important to see brother and sister in everybody, and to see the same longing for beauty and life in everybody, even in the "worst" of people. You know even when I was alive, I had compassion for the soldiers in Bosnia. I thought about them and felt the agony, what they were going through to become such unfeeling, cruel young men. What in all the world is happening to their souls? In a time, when love is so abundant, the hate and the indifference try to show their ugly faces to keep themselves a little more alive. This will be resolved. They will be replaced. Hate and destruction cannot be victorious, never, because life feeds everything and God‘s spirit IS in everything and around all, so how could destruction win. It cannot – because it is not real, it is not the reality of life, not the true reality. Think of that ...

My deepest wish would be, that people have a new purpose for what they do. You know there are some who came here and went back into the life on Earth – and started to live a different, more essential life. To live a life with the REAL values – love, caring, intimacy, thankfulness, integrity, closeness, compassion, forgiveness, pools of light to bathe in. Yes, to bathe in. It is like water, which washes all the dirt from you – this light is a cleansing light.

All these people who came here and went back to life, who went from life to life, so to speak, are they not saying, that they focus on the essential now?

So focus on the essential, my friends. Those who do movies – and you know whom I mean – Steven, Tom, Dustin and all those I love, try to focus on the essential. Your power is so immense. You can reach the deepest in people. Why do you think that you have this power of money and fame? What messages do you transport?

Much is given to you ...

2nd October 1997

I was not murdered. This is a string you should not follow up on. Once again I say this: all is perfect. It was a shock for the physical Diana, but it is not a shock for me, with the name Diana that I had in this lifetime. Yes, I lost a child – but the soul of this child was not harmed. She will come in another time and still complete her mission. She was a token for the love between Dodi and me, for the promise – a new promise – between a man and a women. It is somewhat strange: so much desire between men and women in the world, and so much fear between them. There is also so much violence, so much misunderstanding, and so much separation between them because of fear. My life with Dodi was completely without fear. I felt so light with him, so easy – and not because of his wealth with which he could fulfil my every wish, but because of the strength of his heart and the knowing, that everything is possible – even the easy playful joyful love between man and woman.

Yes, there is a tendency in the world of this ending 20th Century to fight all that which is supposed to come. Those who are suffering the most are the children – watch out for the children. They are the bearers of the mysteries of the new age, of the next centuries. In many ways they hold the mirror up where you see yourselves. They bring the purity which is so important for the times to come. They are the vision bearers – so take care of the children. Give them healthy food to think, to watch and to learn. Give them the warmth in the families they so desperately need. Give them a home – not only a house.

In my travels I realized that all the homeless are not the problem – they are made into the problems. They stand for the inner homelessness of people. The sick and the poor of this world show the sickness and poverty in the people's hearts. If you care for the sick and the poor, the cast outs, then you do something for your own sick and homeless soul. Everything which is shown outside is also inside. The Earth is suffering and she must heal, and she is going to new dimensions.

Even as a child I thought about the strange fact that there is so much sadness in the world. I saw the beauty of trees, of the sky, of water and the animals, the butterflies, the birds – and then I also saw the pain in the people – especially in the adults. There were times when I told myself that I did not ever want to grow up. I did not want to enter the world of the adults. What good would it do and be – to be one of them?

Yet still, one grows up – and most times one forgets the troubles of childhood – and there are more troubles than most people think. I swore to myself always to be there for children – especially for my own but also for the children in general. I never lost the connection to childhood even though it was as bleak as it was – but I never lost the connection. In my childhood dreams and also as a teenager I told myself not to forget the feelings I had had as a child, the joys, the exitements and the pains and the losses. I wanted to be somebody who remembers, who says: "Yes, I know how you feel ...".

As a kindergarden teacher I felt that I was among my own kind. I loved the work. I loved my children, and they loved me. I remember one little girl who often came to me and looked at me with her big blue eyes and said: "Mummy, are you o.k.?" Why she said: "Mummy"- I do not know, but it is true, I was often sad even then, because this very girl was an orphan, living with her grandmother, who was very hard on her. She always trembled when she was picked up after kindergarden. Me a mummy? Yes, how much I wanted to be one, and to give my children all the love and care children very often do not get.

I often also dreamed of a kingdom of children – a place were children are amongst each other and remain as children. I knew of course that everybody grows up and that this is the course of time – but what I felt is that many problems would disappear if people would only remember their childhoods more – in some sense continueing to be children. I could not see enough pictures of mummies and children who were hugging and cuddling, being so much at one and in tune with each other.

I knew Charles loved my way with children. He watched it often, and I saw this glow on his face and in his eyes, and I saw him become tender. I had always been full of hope that when he had children, he would let me have them, keep them, and educate them. I had hoped he would resist the regulations and the royal rules for his children's sake. Of course I knew of the way royals normally were educated, but I had had this hope, that Charles would intervene if they tried to take the children away and put them in those schools. He did not. He was rather angry with me, the one "who never grew up". I could not believe that he had forgotten his own despair when he was a child, but apparently this is the difference: some remember, some not, and some never want to. His childhood was worse than mine, much worse. I at least had a father who, in between his emotional imbalances, gave me space to be who I am. He knew of his mistakes and failures so I could make mistakes, whereas at the court I needed to be perfect.

They were not perfect, no, I saw things, I felt things beyond their perfection which were full of despair, full of decay and crying out for life. Whenever I was at Buckingham my body felt as though it were weighed down by thousands of pounds. I felt heavy. I could not eat. I could hardly walk upright. How can they live there? I wondered.

At the beginning of our marriage Charles was the only one – sometimes Fergie as well – but mainly Charles who was a ray of sun in these dark chambers. I thought as long he is on my side, nothing bad can happen, as through him and in our love there was always a fresh breath in the palace.

The Queen was finally stronger, his mother in himself. He felt with her all the time. He felt with her and not with me. He felt her agony and tried to ease her pain. There was this bond – it seemed to be very old, probably from his childhood, a weight he took on his shoulders then, to carry something for his mother – the weight of a king. It was something like: "I hope, my son, that whatever I will be unable to do as a queen, you will do as a king". She trusted him. He was her vision. So at the beginning I was the perfect wife for Charles, because I seemed to be easily controlled. I always agreed in the early days – that is true. I nodded, I said yes. It was like a child starting to play a role in a drama and there are the directors and assistants telling you what to do, because they know the piece. Therefore of course one does what they say, because you do not know what to do. Certainly I came from a well accepted house and family – so everything seemed to be perfect, but I could not play my role well. It was like – even funny – being a main actor and at the same time moving something around in the background. Now I was supposed to stay in the background where no light would shine on me inspite of being a main actor. It did not work. Wherever I went on this stage, the bright light shone on me. This was not because I wanted or needed it – but because I apparently was the only one who reflected the light.

When Charles and I walked together, we both reflected the light. I shone light on him, and it reflected. I was so proud of him at times.

Then came these nagging doubts, doubts about his love.

It was ironic and sad as well – in many ways the photographers, the media helped me to get out of my thoughts, doubts and despair. Yes, it is true, at one point of my life at the court I turned around and showed them my face. I said to myself: I am naked and stripped in the background, then I can be naked and stripped in front of everybody as well. If I hide, I will die. So I might as well go forward – maybe this will shake them up. Of course there was always the question what will I do as the Princess of Wales? What will I do at the side of Charles? Will I hold myself back? Shall I push the lamps on his face? Shall I point to him? Shall I just be a good modest wife?

I tell you, I wanted to be that!

I was surprised myself that I started to love publicity, the public love and attention which was given to me. It was not as they are saying in the newspapers now, that I wanted vindication towards the Windsors. No. It was more that I started to feel I was loved. Yes it is true, the love of the public at times eased the painful love between Charles and myself. How can I describe it – there was Diana, having cried the whole night, with red wrinkled eyes, knowing there would be a day, where people, who did not know anything about what I was going through, would want to see me – either directly or indirectly through the photographs of the so called paparazzi. So I got out of bed, I dressed carefully, I pulled myself together, I did the façade Diana and became Diana again, through the help of this photographed façade. Yet I was not the façade anymore. I pushed myself to the first and then to the second smile, and then I smiled, and then I was there, and then I felt alive. I needed it at one point, I needed this being tracked, trapped and taken, if not in my marriage – then at least in public.

From 1985 on it was my children who gave me the love back and all the attention. From this time on I started to hate to be "shot", and to be tracked everywhere I went. Somehow the desire for privacy came back into my life through my children. They did not need this kind of obtrusive flashlight attack and I did not want it for them. It is – it feels like being stripped, it does literally, and exiting as it can be to be haunted and to play hide and seek, it did not feel exiting for them.

So I started to become very protective, but it was too late. I had gone too far. There were photographers and media people with whom I already had a strange intimate relationship. It was like a co-dependency which I did not want any longer. So suddenly I pushed them back and they could and would not understand. Even my resistance seemed to make them and the public even hungrier, and from then on I understood a terrible truth: People feed on the lives, the crises and the despairs of others. Suddenly all that which I had innocently seen as love and attention felt ugly, like sticky fingers reaching into my very guts. Well maybe I would have taken it – but not my children. They had not done anything. If I had lost my innocence, I still wanted them to keep theirs.

Some religions do not allow photographing people. You know why? Because the image of God is holy – and an image is the door to the essence of a person.

When I started to retreat from the media and was unable to shut the door ... this was the time of Charles. He had warned me many times to be more careful, to retreat, to resist more – and now he came with his: "See, I told you so ... You brought those vultures into our family."

I felt very bad, and very guilty. See, in my naivity I considered that all those media people were my friends. I thought that those who would take note when I was open and accessible would also show understanding when I wanted my privacy and desired to be in a safe protected space. At times – and they made me feel it – I thought they would take part of my joy and happiness and love – and I wanted them to have it.

The horrible thing was now, no matter what the circumstances were – they still smiled and pushed the button. I started to realize that I had been their possession. I could not believe it but it was true: I was public property, they had a right to own me, and therefore my children as well. My God, what have I done, what have I allowed.

But it was not only the media who were creeping into my life everywhere. It was also those I will not name here, the insiders, the grey emminences, those controllers in court who were creeping into the most private spaces – everywhere. They were even in our bedroom, so to speak, from the beginning.

They saw everything, they reported everything, they knew everything, they interpreted everything, and they made suggestions about what to do with me. They gave those slimy hints – even to the press –, these little coldblooded reports how often I had eaten, whom I had called, what the message was, who and what would probably be my next mistake. This slimy insider spying and reporting was more embarassing, more hurtful and more dangerous, than these open media people. One at least knew what they were after. I never was clear what those grey – and yes so friendly – spies were after – they certainly did not want our marriage to work. Why? At times I thought, and later it became obvious, that there were other interests beyond the interests of the royal family. There was no royal family. I say it cautiously and mildly. There were movements and individuals connected to the Queen and her counsellors, who had and have completely different motives than to keep the monarchy alive. I did not understand it then, but I understand more now.

In those days I always thought: 'Why are they doing that? Why are they talking about all those things which make the gap between Charles and myself even deeper?' Those very people who were intimate friends and counsellors – I thought if they insist so much on having the best motives to save our marriage and our reputation, why then are they always putting oil on the fire to make our lives even more difficult and thus increasing strife and discord in our family?

There are forces who want something completely different from family peace – and they definitely did not want ME at the court. I was a mistake – and my mistake was – I was not to be controlled – but it seemed at the beginning that I was the easiest wife to control that a Windsor had ever had.

I want to say here: death cannot see life, but it can detect its traces and try to wipe them out, when they are seen. And my life and aliveness was seen by the eyes of the people who love me – and it still is.

So I was dangerous – and I am even more dangerous now — for them. There will be times when you will know who "they" are, but watch out – they are not in the public eye, but they creep into the homes of all those who want life and to live a free and uncontrolled life. These are the dangerous ones you have to watch out for. Even in my late days so to speak, I still could talk to the paparazzi and still had fun at times. They were alive in their obstruviness and in their stubborn boldness. Well, sometimes I was very angry even furious with them. I shouted at them and they cried. I could have smashed their cameras so easily, and at times their eyes DID look like vultures' eyes, as though they were always smelling where a wounded or dead body lies – but still – it was all obvious, they were visible.

There was a book that I loved very much, "Momo". Just read it again, and you will know.

They, the grey ones, did not cause my death – no, but they made it very hard for me to live – yes. And nobody seemed to detect them – and they always seemed to have the best motives.

Dodi and his family were my big protection – and I needed this sense of protection before I went. I needed to know, that there was somebody rich and powerful — and good-hearted. He was, he is good-hearted. A clean, good-hearted character: open, vulnerable, tender and loving. He smelled death long before it came and he avoided it. In that tunnel – as strange as it sounds – Dodi and I went for life.

It was a tunnel ... remember? A tunnel always leads to something new. We did not get stuck there, believe us! We are more alive than ever before, and ... yes, unchecked and uncontrolled – – – with very few heavenly paparazzis.

Dodi does not want to talk in this book, and I respect his decision. He might do it at another time or place.

Nature. Something about nature. From my perspective here it is so beautiful that you have nature. It is being so close to creation. It makes you feel that you are alive and that you are a part of creation. In these cities – it does not matter if east or west – I often felt the heaviness of being imprisoned in places without nature. Smog makes it even worse – and smog is not only the emanations from machines, road traffic or industry – but smog is also what is emanating from people. This heaviness really can be lifted by being in nature. I loved being in nature with Charles and the children – in the early times. Whenever we have been in nature things were somewhat better between us. Also in the "end times" when we did the walks with the children or went to places in Scottland and Wales and elsewhere, we got on better with each other in nature. Nature helps, nature lifts. Nature is the most beautiful gift of God and a great healer of body, soul and spirit. In nature you return to yourself, to your origin. You feel yourself again ... who you really are.

It is also important to love your body, the nature of your body. I always strived hard to love my body – I did excessive sports – I trained it – this was a way to feel good, to feel alive. When I was in nature – really close to water and air – my eating behaviour was much easier to handle. Often I forgot all about it. I was just eating and drinking what I wanted and got. In addition I always liked good fresh water from wells. Water, water ... in any form.

It is significant that I felt my first really strong feelings to Charles when he taught me swimming. This was our element ... this was the royal element ... water – and it is! We both liked nature, liked water, and fresh air – it was an element of our love.

My sickness – bulimia – seldom ocurred when I was outside – it mainly struck me, when I followed my royal duties – the banquettes were horrible, the kitchen seemed to be lifeless ... my body could not hold the food behind those walls – there was no place to digest it ... because there was nothing to digest. All those women stricken by this sickness, I want to tell you – go into nature, drink clear fresh water where you can find it, have fun with waves, have fun with sun and air. Have fun with yourselves ... do not try to fit in, as I did or at least tried to. My body did not like to fit in .. so it bounced between craving and letting go, trying to find a way out ... so do your bodies. Give your bodies a way out – into nature, into meeting your very own creation, having fun with yourselves, jump and dance.

If you can, go to places with dolphins. I saw many dolphin shows and I even went to the ocean to see dolphins jump and swim – they were like me. My "Spencer special" was a dolphin jump – to jump as dolphins do – elegantly, smoothly, without splashing too much water. If you can ... swim with dolphins. They have the spirit of the closeness to nature, the closeness to their existence, the closeness to creation. You cannot stay sad and depressed while swimming with dolphins or even when watching them jump ... feel like a dolphin, and you feel better.

By the way the dolphins told me, that they do NOT LIKE to be in small basins, that they really suffer, even if people do not see it, and it does not show. They mention in particular that basins filled with chlorine water are terribly damaging – especially to the fine senses of their noses, and also to their skin. When some of them jump more than others in these basins, it is not because they like the show, but because each jump is a moment of release from that water, a moment of freedom. Dolphins love people, but this is not the way they want to love them or be loved by them.

Really, I would like to come again as a dolphin or a whale. Wasn't I the Princess of Whales? (She is laughing). But I will not.

Britain, England, I love you. I love all of you dearly, and in my heart I will always reserve a place for you. Children of England I love you. Children of England take heart and courage – build the new country, preserve the hills, the parks, and the resorts. Be golden children, magical, and wonderful. Be joyful, dance and sing. Be lights in the world. All of you who came to put the flowers down, your poems, your pictures, I saw each one of you, Bob and Mary, Julian and Gary, Sarah and Philip, – and all of you in France, in Germany, in Poland, in Bosnia and Croatia and all the other countries- you Mirjam, you Peter, you Sybil and Ursula, you Mirko, Tanja, all you – I saw your tears, I saw and felt your love. I touched your arm, I touched your hair, even when you went into this Chapel and prayed for me, Susan, I was with you. I heard your words, I saw your tears. You people throughout the world I saw each one of you! You know, one can do this from here – one sees differently, one sees it all, one has "all the time". What a joy, what a jubilant time for me. I felt nothing was in vain. I really felt like a princess floating above these flowers – did you feel my smile, my laughter, my peace and my freedom? Did you feel it in Kalkutta, in Los Angeles, in Tel Aviv and Gaza, did you experience it in Cairo and Amsterdam, in Rio and Hong Kong?

If only, if only my so often quoted smile could make you smile. I want you to smile. My smile will fade throughout the years, but your smiles you can renew, each and every day. Give your smiles to others. Smile at yourselves, smile at your children, and smile to the old, a smile from the heart, and a smile of tenderness and compassion.

Charles, my brother! Charles, beloved, oh beloved – my dearest. I heard you, I stood beside you – if only we could have been that which we were then for each other while I was still around. I know, it was difficult for you to understand my ways. I really loved what you said – you spoke so much out of my own heart, and my heart was with you.

If there were any possible way I would love it if you and Charles could understand each other, especially regarding the children, so that hat they could be in Althorp as often they want to be there.

My spirit is with you Charles. Think of the times we played, we played King and Queen, we played fairy tales and our fantasy games. Remember when we built those towers and houses for the sick and poor, and the rich and hard, the heroes and the black riders.

Be with William – tenderly – because he has many things to overcome. At times I was not the mother I wanted to be for him and he – he felt the danger, and the risks I was taking. He wanted to grow up in a safe world which I could not provide.

I do not talk about bodygards, I do not talk about this kind of safety. I talk about the safety of a family which is whole and complete. This he did get, but only for a short time.

What can I tell you, William? The only thing I can tell you is that I tried, and when you are older, you will find out for yourself the intricacies of life. I was always so proud of you, yes, you my big boy.

In your smile I saw mine, in your hands, which were so tenderly holding this sick child, I saw my own. The words you have spoken to this ill girl, you have spoken out of my heart. Whatever I can do I will do for you, and I will ask all the angels to protect you and especially to protect your heart.

Also I always want to ask you for forgiveness for when I have not been the mother, you needed – and I trust you feel my love. Keep your smile, my son, keep your smile, and your good heart.

Harry, my beloved, my beloved child, laughing and playing, stick to it. Create more of your wonderful inventions, machines, waterpipes, cars, solar mobiles, houses and architectures – show them what can be done. Keep Daddy's heart strong.

About where I am now, you ask? This is a delightful and blissful place ... yes it is. I can see the essence of everything, I can see the spirit of God in everything, in every tree, in every stone and in the water. This is all so original, and intact. It is not intact in your mind – nor was it in mine, but it is now. It is beautiful. If I could just show you the beauty – the beauty of everything. Yes, God IS. And He is different. He is not a religious God, He is not even a „He". But „He" is personal – and humorous and such a smile. That is why smiling comes directly from God, the true and wonderful smile of a child. The smile of a baby.

How much I have loved the first smile of William, the first smile of Harry. How much I loved Charles' smile, when he touched my hand or my hair.

How many lifetimes I had envisioned this wedding ceremony. I had seen the pictures over and over again. I had practiced – I wanted to fulfil the dream of dreams, a marriage which would go around the world, a marriage which would talk of love, and about everything which can be possible between a man and a woman, a Prince and a Princess, and Queen and a King. I wanted to show that there is Royalty, a Royalty which can be seen and shown, as a token, a symbol of the beauty of mind and heart, of the ultimate dream which it is possible to live and experience. It was as though I were in trance. It seemed to be taken out of my hands. It just happened. There were so many who smiled at me, truly wanted the best for me, to make me happy, and to give me a place of beauty. I felt so loved. I was so exited. The shadows of the preceding days vanished completely. There was only Charles, my Charles, my eternal man, and myself. We mattered, we loved each other, and we were loved. I felt the warmth of the millions of people, I felt their hearts beating, I felt their tears of being moved, their good wishes, and prayers.

This "I" was the shy one, and there was this strength in me, when I was Charles's wife. I felt it so strongly, that I wanted to make him proud of me, and to stand up for this love in front of everybody. My "Yes" was a clear yes. It was given to the Charles he was at that moment. I saw the sparkle in his eyes, his face clear and strong. All the sorrow which was usually on his face, was wiped away. There was the picture I had seen all the time of the man I had envisioned for years, over lifetimes.

I knew he deserved this moment of celebration and bliss. We both deserved it – and we knew it. We were like islands in the storm as we held each others hands, looked at each other, and we encouraged one another. This was Charles, beyond all the boundaries and rules, strong and tender, showing his true character, his essence. Oh, how I loved him, how I love him still. How much I wanted him to be this man – full of Charisma, strength, loving care, tenderness, vulnerability and Majesty. He has every quality of a king – yes. If he just dares ... if he just dares to believe that the people need heart-felt love not ceremonies, that they need deeds not words, that they need the warmth of a warm body – not a walking monologue.

People want to relate. They want the genious and they want the relationship. They want to see and to be seen. They want to prepare for the new times to come. They want security, safety, they want a role model, they want somebody they can look up to, not in a devotee way, but somebody who can show them, that there is light, the light on the horizon where life goes on.

I knew how much people needed to trust in the future. I always trusted in the future, and that things would become better. Even in my deepest despair, I knew there was always a way out, always love and a life to be experienced. I did not want to wallow too long in a pain, a worry or sorrow. I knew it would make me sick, and whenever I did, it did make me sick. Whenever I came to a point where I did not know how to get further, I saw somebody smiling, somebody who reminded me of .. well, of the ONE, the spark, the life – and I saw it often in men.

When I saw this particular smile, this particular vitality and tenderness I was gone. I grabbed it, I took hold of it – it was my kind, it was a part of me. That is why it was so painful, like the disappointments with James for instance. In the beginning of our secret love I saw in him what I had lost in Charles and did not seem to find anymore. It was not done out of vindictiveness. It was not to give him, Charles, a lesson because of Camilla. No, I wanted to complete the picture of my life again. Here I found something in James which I had lost in Charles.

I know now that this was not a responsible act – not at all. I hurt Charles, I hurt James, but most of all I hurt myself. An expression of this hurt was the way James turned round and betrayed everything which was between us. Yes, he was a deep love – and in some ways he saved my life, but it would not have happened at all, if Charles and I could have shared what we promised each other we would share.

I was hungry and thirsty. I was greedy for life – yes, wherever I could see it, whenever I could hold a warm body or give warmth – this was also true in my intimate life.

Please understand all you so well educated and good people – there is something in all of "us" which demands life and you need to hear this voice. If you hear this voice and you give it space you can stop wars. Wars, rape, violence would no longer be there or necessary because life would abound. Violence is the result of apathy and frustration. If there is apathy, if there is no perspective in life, if there is no vision, there is violence. What can give people more vison and more life than the love between man and woman. It is lifegiving – literally. It was given and meant for this from the beginning.

So focus, you women and focus you men on a new kind of relationship and intimacy. Be thankful for each other. Eagerly and quickly forgive one another. Let the bitterness and resentment go. Look at the preciousness of your togetherness. Look out for what you have in common, what you share, and do not look at these things which separate you. Do not make a dogma out of your love – keep it fresh, keep it vital, keep it with a sense of laughter and with humor. Let go of old beliefs as much and fast as possible.

I speak of old beliefs which hold people in the prisons of their minds and dictate their actions. People of Northern Ireland, end it! Let the weapons drop. Your strife is born out of an old misunderstood desperate love for one another. You do not know how to live. If you knew who God is, and what true Christianity would be, if only you would turn to the religion of your heart, you would end this craziness. You old frustrated warriors, hear your people! Yes, you have people, yes, you have wives, mothers, fathers and babies. Listen to your babies cry and to their laughter. Let your hearts be softened, open your eyes to the beauty of your country. If you ever have loved me, if you ever considered my person as somebody who knows something about people and their striving for life – let them live. Let yourselves live. Your are not too old, you are not too hard, you still have hearts which are beating in your breasts. You still have sons and daughters for whom you want the best of life. I mean both of you – protestants and catholics. Yes, there is only ONE God, and He laughs about all dogmas and forms, for He is not in them. He is not in religions-never was and never will be.

What you carry is all empty like shoe boxes without anything more hiding inside them than the dust of centuries. It is the dust of death which creates death.

3rd October 1997

What is truly of value? What is worth living for? I learn, I go on learning, and the learning never ends. Where I am, it is a place of contemplation, learning, and evaluation. It is a crowded place.

Here are many, many of whom I talk with, and share what I have seen and learned. Also I still go around visiting those I have loved. The first truth about life and death which struck me is that they are so close – they are imbedded in each other. Life and death are not separate. There is life beyond life, yes. It is like going through a door into something you always know and always knew.

The process of dying is not necessarily such fun, this is true.

For me it was in many ways terrible ... looking into these faces who only wanted to see me die. What did you want to see? Who was I for you at that moment? Who at all understood who I was and why I came?

For each of you I am a challenge! Who would have liked to be in my place – with my wretched body, torn in warped metal – with all my bones broken – knowing that one cannot fix it, that it is beyond any help, and yet they still push their buttons. You see the sweat on their faces, you see the horror in their eyes and the greed – these were seconds and they were very long. I could not believe what I saw and experienced, but I UNDERSTOOD. With it I understood all of the tragedy – the tragedy of being alienated from feelings, and from life itself.

If you are so close to death you should feel life even more intensely, but if you are always reading and watching TV about life and do not live it – then death also will be something which you will not understand.

But then you understand ... Some of those who were at the place of the accident ... they suddenly understood ... and they took their understanding, the shock of understanding home with them – home to their families, home to their partners, maybe even home into bars and places of blind pleasure. All of you ... if you cannot say what you have seen ... then learn. Learn that you have seen life ... you have seen a naked body, torn, smashed ... and you saw I was still there ... and I am. Did this not push you into your life ... to see who YOU are? The beauty and yes ... also the ugliness, how uncompassionate and how greedy you are? Could this be a moment of thinking about yourself, a moment of purification ... like the torch of fire I have been. Yes, maybe a candle, but also fire. I am fire!

You so called paparazzi, you are the mirror of so many. You are the ones who have the courage to go close to what is happening, you jump into life and you jump into death – and I felt you are my allies and often you have been, you were my channels by which I could express myself ... so, do you have the courage to tell, what you have seen and felt? I saw your tears, I saw your agonies, I saw your excuses and your good intentions ... the agonies of your soul while you made and sold those photos. Whatever you do with them ... know that I am not this anymore. I was not in this crushed body, and I was not in my corpse in Westminster – I was free already ... much freer than I ever have been.

And Dodi was with me ... my love.

I felt more shame for you than my pain at that moment. When the car crashed it was such an impact, it was such a shock – a shock through all my existences. I felt violated, I felt raped by the torn metal in my body, by the impact of the crash, and the physicalness of this reality.

Minutes before when I felt the arm of Dodi, when he was holding me – it felt like flying after being in the Ritz. I was so happy, the glass of wine had made me feel light. I was floating on that cloud of happiness, with him, a flight into the sky of happiness, into the heavens of bliss.

Then the car skidded ...

Trevor tried to calm Henri down, but he was in a mood to show them, to show the world what he could do. He seemed to be proud to be able to demonstrate how he can transgress every boundary, every limit ... and he did. No other would have done it. He could do it ... and something inside us knew it, and he knew ... days and weeks beforehand.

While he was driving after some time I felt a dread, I felt that there was something very wrong. The car did not move as usual – it started to roll, to sway. It did not feel right and I grabbed Dodi's arm. I felt it, and so did he. In those seconds which became slower somehow I sensed that something very terrible was going to happen, something completely out of my control. I was clear and sober in an instant – and I knew, it was the end. I knew it seconds and eternities before it happened. I looked at Dodi. He was screaming something to Henri – and Henri – – – Henri was laughing. It was so strange – here we were in this car – the last seconds – and I saw the REALITY of everything. Nothing could be stopped, nothing could be done. I saw this pillar come towards us, I heard the crash, I felt this terrible impact and then it was as though we were in a roller coaster, everything turned – I felt this being in the hand of a huge mighty power beyond my reach, beyond any control. In such a moment you try to deny what happens, you want it to be a strange dream of some sort, – but it was MY body which was shaken and torn, smashed between the crushing interiors of that heavy car.

And ... it felt familiar, as if I have experienced it all before ...

When it was calm I saw myself from above, hanging out of one of the windows of that pile of rubble. Then I saw myself. I was not bleeding. I was torn out of my body and slowly went back, and then I was in my body, and a flashlight exploded in my face. At that moment I felt this terrible pain in my breast and abdomen, I felt my heart beating so fast, and I could not breathe. When I took a breath, it was a pain like thousands of knives cutting through me. So I decided to go out of my body again, while somewhat bewildered I looked at all the people who were running around the car, and all the time even new people were arriving. I had the feeling, all this was a long practised drama of some sort – and they were the actors who had learned their role.

At that moment I thought of Dodi. What a shock! I tried to look at him, – but I could not turn. I could not look inside the car. I just heard people saying – "There is the other one, oh God", somebody said, and another "... Is this Dodi Al-Fayed...?" It was another enormous shock. It was all over.

Then I remembered that day and the preceding days, the happiness, the laughter, the tenderness between us, and even the wonderful moments we had had at the Ritz, where Dodi asked me ... and I said yes.

In the minutes and hours after the crash, when time was still relevant, I went in and out of my body. Somehow I wanted to help the doctors and the ambulance. Even then I wanted to make them happy by letting them see me move, just to give them a little hope. I told one of them that I was pregnant, – and I saw this look on his face – the deepest expression of compassion I have ever seen on a man.

Nonetheless I wanted to go, because I had seen that Dodi had gone. He was already beside me. There was a moment of hesitation, and there was a moment of –

maybe I should go back, but I considered all the consequences and the fact that I would have to leave Dodi. This I did not want – and when the light came, it was completely clear to me that everything was perfect. I surrendered ...

Dear ones ... all of you who hear and read this! Hear it even louder in your hearts! It is important to live. Stay alive, stay in the places where you are. Everybody has another purpose in life, everybody has another plan. Do not think it is heroic to forget about life on the beautiful planet Earth and leave. You see, my life was complete, even though you do not think it was.

But your life is not complete yet... even though you might think it is .... even if you might think you cannot stand life anylonger, as I thought so many times ... at 6, at ten, at 14, and at 33 years old and the many times in between ... It is understandably so – because if you are a child of the New Age, if you are a tender one, a compassionate one, a person with a heart and life ... then the longing for freedom in another life form is very close.

That is because you remember. You remember that there is a state of being free of all pain, and this is true. The irony of it is, however, that you can only die with that bliss, with that feeling of going home, after you have really lived. Life on planet Earth is important and you have a task to do. There is so much to accomplish, therefore do not be words only, but let your deeds follow. Visit the sick and the poor. Heal with love those who are desperate, those who are sick ... even if you think it is their own fault. Give away your smiles, and happiness will be in your heart and a real sense of life.

You know, I always had my head bent to one side. I was always asking ... I always asked, what is the truth here and how can I love? And I am also asking while I look at you ... will you give something from yourself? Will you be generous with your love and with your heart?

Do you know? Even the mightiest of this world are crying out for love ... because when you die there is only ONE question: Have I loved enough? And if you had much to give, money, or influence ... your next question will be: How did I use my wealth and my power?

What will you do with all the money? I often thought about the mighty and rich of the world. Why do they forget what good they could do with their wealth?

I was very moved by the number of people who sent the smallest amounts to help me with my organizations. Many were there who had nearly nothing to give – and they gave. Do you know, how much money is needed to feed a child for a whole year – in Africa, in Indonesia, or in Asia? Ten, twenty pounds? Do you know about the millions and billions of pounds which are sitting somewhere in banks, in savings, in stocks, shares and bonds, or in real estate – which do nothing but grow? Grow where? Grow what? They grow, these tons of piled up money – while those who really should grow are dying! This does not make any sense from here.

Everything that is stuck does not move. Hearts are moving, hearts are against stuckness ... the spirit of God is like a wind trying to move everything if you just let yourself move. The spirit of God is not something on a guarded mountain or in a far off heaven – no, the spirit of God is right inside your heart and wants to move there, wants to breathe, wants to live and grow – so, give the blood of your riches and wealth – in any form – a way to flow. Let the blood of compassion flow throughout all your world and it will even appease vulcanoes, it will stop the outside fires if you are ready to let the fires of your hearts burn. The Earth just shows you what is happening in your hearts – the Earth's tears are her floods, the Earth's unfulfilled passions are her fires and the Earth's desiring expressions of her very soul are the eruptions of her vulcanoes. If you retreat out of fear, frustration or slowness of your mind, the Earth reacts. The Earth is the field of your dreams. She shows what you are.

The Earth trembled. It trembled because of you and me. I was a real queen – and I felt as such – I was connected to each of your hearts – shy little Diana ... Diana, the one who knows that love moves mountains. Yes, I wanted to become queen, and now I am – I have fulfilled my mission – I gave you the royalty back – a royalty with all the failures and mistakes that I have had and made, and with all of my passions and intentions. I was queen of your hearts not your minds. You identify yourself so much with your minds ... minds abound and minds die. It will not, however, be the mind which will govern the next centuries – HEARTS and SPIRIT will lead into the new time – and you have chosen. Yes all of you, all those who were with me, who felt the connection, all those who secretly cried, all you, who were more loving to your parents, to the sick and feeble, to the homeless, all you, who have laid down the flowers at the palaces of tradition to make them into palaces of the future – all you have decided that the Earth will live! It was an answer to all those who predicted and predict the end, who predicted that love and compassion will be replaced by frustration, destruction and death. The answer is: No, LOVE IS. Love is and it will prevail, always, eternal – because love is the material of which the Earth is made.

So – do not forget. Keep the testimony of my life. It is not about me ... you might forget me and my life throughout the years ... you do not need to remember me and what you felt about me, but remember what you have felt about YOURSELVES when you laid down the flowers at Kensington, in the tunnel, and at places around the world. Remember what has moved in your hearts when you watched or visited the funeral, and when you heard the speeches, the choir and the songs.

There was a reason that I came as a woman.

All you women I could touch, – remember your strength. Remember your power, your good power – remember what you felt and feel – yes, you are important, you are the saviours of the world – you will tear down the walls and you need courage. Cry, yes, and then smile. Open your mouth – open your eyes. Stop the darkness, stop the stuckness – let the lifeblood of power, money and good works flow to the places of sadness and despair. Let nobody remain unfed whom you can feed. It does not take a lot, you do not have to become Queen or Popess. No, you can work from where you are. Women of the world, create the network of your hearts – stop the wars, stop the insanities of those who cannot and never want to live. Women, my friends, you are the bearers of life – so be it. Demonstrate it ....

There ARE men who listen! Dodi was, is one of them. His life was not perfect, he was seeking, he was running his life as everybody else does, and bounced from one side to the other as everyone does, but he had the heart of a man who knows how to be with a woman, how to respect her power, her passion and the life bearing body. So you men, liberate the female souls in you, the ones who understand, because the female is in you too. There is so much of it in Charles, and in William and Harry. It is so abundant in all those men who know about the whisper of the soul.

You are so well known, you artists of the world, musicians, poets, writers, screen writers, movie producers ... fill the gap with life! Fill it with love and values. You know how to do it.

You also know how to describe the wrongs and failures, the wars and destructions. To go on describing them and to manifest those patterns over and ove is as antiquated as the dinosaurs.

Over and over again people watch those destructive movies, read those articles and books. Children, the smallest of them, still in their cradles, are surrounded by these pictures. They are surrounded by these electronic thoughts and images which work their way into their minds and souls all the time.

Small children with their receptive and eager brains consume everything that they can get hold of ... because they want to learn. Children want to learn ... and it is your responsiblity what they learn ... what they see and receive ... directly and indirectly each and every day.

Wake up, people! Go for life – go for the goodness! Many people throughout different lands and countries do not have work and jobs. This is a sign ... so do works of love! Even if you do not have a job ... that does not mean that you are without work. There are thousands of possibilites and ways in which you CAN DO things. Yes it is so, and it must be that way. The old ways of living and working are over.

There are new jobs to be invented ... in hospitals, nursing homes, on the streets, in laboratories, in service – do serve your neighbour! O yes, many jobs can be created which are based on love and care ... and they are waiting to be taken. How many people helped to remove the tons of flowers? How many people are there, who had a temporary job, because those flowers had to be picked, delivered, wrapped and sold? How many more jobs were created out of the love for me? Can you not love somebody else now and continue to have work???

Give flowers – in any form – to those who really need them.

How willing was the Earth to give all these flowers – and have you been willing to thank the Earth?

The Earth is willing, are you?

Yes it is like an ongoing theme – and I had already thought about it early in my life. Everything seemed to be either sourced by indifference, hatred or darkness or it seemed to be originate from love and the eagerness for peace, creation, laughter, and fun. Very early on I looked into the faces of others, other children, adults, old people, even into the faces of animals – and I wondered why they looked so sad. I wanted to change that – I wanted to bring laughter to the people and joy – I wanted to see how this sadness stopped, and how it could be replaced by joy. Seeing pictures of war, especially when children were involved was very terrible for me. There were times when I doubted I was on the right planet.

On the other hand in my relationship to nature and my animals, and with the fun I had with my sisters and friends I thought life was good, and beautiful. But I could not understand how people could mistreat children and animals... It shook me deep inside, as I felt the coldness which creeps here from a source I could neither understand nor explain.

This kind of thinking and considerations dominated my whole life. When I saw pictures of war and of destruction, I thought to myself, are these soldiers not sons of mothers, are they not fathers of children? Is it so hard for them to draw the conclusion that what they sow now one day they will reap? I learned that in the Kindergarden, I learned it from the Bible. Everywhere it is said – and they act, as though it were not so.

Yet it is said in every religion. I could not believe that people could quarrel because of religious differences. There are only people — only!

So I discovered over the years that there are people who feel, who are close to life – and there are those, who are — where? What is wrong with those who can do such terrible things to others? Is not a heart beating in their breasts? What do they want to manifest, to prove, to stabilize?

Then I discovered: there is a force, something in people, which is against life – something dark, something grey and very cold. Something that enjoys the opportunity to hurt, to torture, to make wrong and sick, to imprison – something which is sarcastic, cynical – something without a face – because a face can smile, it can reason, and it can lie – the face. If there is only a façade the words come out of an empty mouth.

Are these people deaf and blind? How much they must hate themselves if they allow and do all this? Where are their souls?

Who is inciting the battles in Bosnia time and time again? Who cannot listen to a begging mother and a whispering child, and who is feeding on all this pain...?

The answer is: indifference. All these things grow on ... indifference, and apathy, which are the true enemies of love. The lack of will to change something, the lack of will to put ones heart where ones mouth is. Indifference is the opposite of love, and its sisters and brothers are fanatism, violence, rape, and carelessness. These can only grow on the soil of the indifference of the people who consume only notes, news and pictures, and do not act in life.

Will it all be forgotten, will you people go back into your apathy? Wash your faces and show them! Help my son William to become the king of hearts. He is not indifferent. He has the seed that I have sown in an hour of love with his father, who has the ingriedient of will. Love and will are combined in William. He has trained his soul and heart for this task for a long time, in many lifetimes. He is willing and open, IF YOU LET HIM, ... and if you support him with your prayers and good thoughts. It is not more about me, it is not more about Charles – we had our chance, and Charles had his chance – it is not more about the Monarchy, not more about the way it can survive. It is about William and all that he stands for ... the synergy of Charles and myself and so much more than the sum of us .

He is, and he will be the role model for many, such as the youth, the people to come – strong in heart and mind, with his true and fearless future oriented charisma. Emotions are a great vehicle for goodness and truth. If you can support William with your emotions, you can support goodness and truth – globally, regionally and in your own homes. Further more the best protection for William IS that you, you who love me, love him, and all that which he represents.

Yes, the times of the old monarchy are over. The monarchy written on a fading paper is burned by the fire of passion. There is nothing to be protected, nothing to watch out for. As colonalism, as borders and walls are broken down, as Europe opens, as the world unites – the old politics will fade and fail, they will lose life and blood. They will neither feed people anymore nor give them jobs or homes. They can go on digging for all the resources of the world and no richness of the world can stop what is coming – a new era and a new kind of monarchy. In this monarchy there will be no „subjects“ anymore, but people, human beings. The royal family are the ones who are royal in their hearts. They will build the new monarchy.

A monarchy as a source of power and love, of strength and wisdom – the wisdom not of an old feeble mind but the wisdom of a brand new spirit, the spirit of a child so to speak. Listen to this child, listen to the child within each of you. It is not so unwise. It has desires – listen to its desires. They are true desires, healthy desires, miraculous desires. A new monarchy with a new heart – for a future bright and wonderful, made by those who are willing to dream and to envision. How much we dreamt, William and I, Harry and I, and all of us together. Fantasy and adventure – these were my daily bread with Charles and my sisters. I was dreaming, daydreaming for hours without sense, without boundaries, and just jumping up and down in ecstasy, dreaming and knowing that those dreams can come true. Let your children have their own dreams and allow them to become true.

Your dreams and visions are powerful, William and Harry and all you Williams and Harrys of the world – children of the world. They are true. If you let go of your anger and sadness that I am no longer wih you in physical form – and when you replace it with the mother you will always have – which is IN YOU – when you have forgiven me for leaving you, and when you have perceived that I have not left you – when you have considered it all, then take heart – then go and be the ones who your father and I HAVE DREAMT you will become in our hours of love.

In addition I want to tell you, that whatever we said, whatever we did and no matter what our comments were in times of hardness or discord – your father and I loved each other deeply and still do. Yes, we are separate, and it seems that we are even further apart now, but actually we are more together now than during the times when we tried to live together. I have finally succeeded to be in a place where I wanted to be – a place in his heart. When you are with him, when you play with him, and when he visits you, then always know, that I am there too, because I slipped into his heart. Yes I did! I sneaked in – and he allowed it. That was a beautiful moment, and it is lasting. It will be there all the time, even when he is angry or seems to be uncaring – it is the truth. I am there, and I am here. Also I am all the fun we had together, at any places where we laughed and giggled. I am there in your aunts and uncles, who have loved me and still love me, and in all the people, who are and will be around you, who loved me. I say that, not because I want to hang over your life as the eternal mother who checks everything, but as a comfort and a promise that you are not alone, and you can talk to me as often as you desire.

And – if you desire – I will answer – in many ways. This is my testimony for you. I am your mummy and always will be.

When Trevor is back in life, when he can communicate – do not insist that he should remember. His memory is sealed. He will not remember. Do not torture him, do not insist. He is a fine man – let him be who he is. He had his role in the whole, and it was not his time. He was buckled up in his safety belt – but we were not.

Do not try to find out whose fault it was. All of you who want a reason, to know who was responsible, and who want to point out a finger, point the finger towards yourselves. There is nothing happening in your world which is not also in you. That is the responsibility you have and this is the power you have, because if it is all you, then you can change it – then you do not act as victims. In many ways I saw myself in the children there, in the old people, the homeless, and the sick. I am glad that I allowed myself times in my life, when I felt the despair which I could then recognize in others and understand.

So do not draw false conclusions, do not try to make up a conspiracy or other stories. Even if you could find one it would not help. It would not bring me back to "life" – and I do not even want to come back, because I AM back to life. I would like to "come back" to my children. That is true.

In the realms where I will linger for a while longer however you see things differently – you see them from a very understanding and kind of higher perspective. You see the weaving of times and circumstances, how and why people are born and die, by this means and that, and circumstance, and how souls come and go. It is different from how we see it all on Earth. There is a deep compassionate understanding here – even humorous, serene, even joyful, safe, and trusting.

So do not make me sad by trying to make others guilty. This is NOT what I want. As I mentioned before, nobody is guilty – but everybody plays a part – even you who read this. For everything and everybody seems to be connected, and woven together. It would even be hurtful to make my death into a subject of strife between Muslims and Christians, between the people who love Dodi's family and those who think they must be British enough to point the finger against them. There is enough strife between nations and between religions already.

What a wonderful chance it could be to forgive and heal. It would wipe out, resolve, appease fundamentalism on all sides. This hurtful fundamentalism is not from God, who is the one and only – who is the light and source of all that is ... fundamentalism with all its ugly and atrocious faces ... a last attempt to stick to the past, to a past of exploitation and oppression, of keeping "the male power" alife and to castrate all creativity and life bearing womenhood and all true man power.

This is why they are especially terrible towards women and children – in Algeria, in Egypt, in Spain, Ireland, Turky, Tibet and other countries. They cannot see life. Fundamentalism hates life and all its forms, and fundamentalism is everywhere, in religions, in politics, in ethnic interests, in ideology, educational forms and ancient state forms, who try to keep their power and have to hurt and murder in their powerlessness. Fundamentalism is always a sign that an old power goes and something new, a love will prevail.

Love is a flood, you cannot stop her – you can direct her, but if you resist her, she will put everything under water, and water is stronger than walls. Tears of love are stronger than shouts of hate. Do not forget this. The tears are wiped here and testimonies are given. Fundamentalism is always against women and children, it is always born out of the fear of the female, that is fear of the goddess.

Men of the world, do you have any idea what it means when a woman loves you? Yes, you in the east and west, and north and south, do you know what she sees when she loves you? Is it not so, that she sees an image of God? Is it not so, that she sees the man who loves, a man who loves himself and the world he is responsible for? It does not matter what position what status or profession he has. Does she not see the one who gives form to her essence? Is she not seeing in him the one, who gives his inner beauty and wealth, his tenderness and his expertise. Does he not give the love to his own soul and to hers? Does he not give the shape of his hands, the beauty of his mouth, the straight and tender look of his eyes? Is he not meant to be safe and secure, knowing that what he does and does not is based on the honesty and integrity of his heart? Is he not the one who incites the fires of passion while in return she ignites his creative fires, thus bringing life and form. Was their ever creation without passion, or passion without creation? Is she not loving your smile, the smoothness of your hair, and the courageous posture of your body? Does she not want to give birth to your genious, and to be intune with your spirit so that her spirit can soar, enabling her to be be a genious? Men, what do you think and feel? Why are you still hiding in your attempts to keep the past alive, hiding behind your manlihood which bears wars, fundamentalism and destruction? Is this the way you are hiding?

And you, my fellow women, how long will you believe it? How long will you let them conceal themselves behind sorrows and worries, the fears of losing territories and not surviving, behind the ancient methods for solving problems – problems which do even not exist? How long will you give your power away? Learn from what I have done. I gave my power away at times, I retreated in bulimia, I have shown my wounds, I have mutilated myself, I have cut my arms and breasts – I did all that, so that you do not need to continue doing it. You do not have to disappear! Stop and resolve the shame of your existence! Be the powerful loving, passionate women you are. Take heart, take courage, not against men but for you and them. Show them who you are, show your power in creating a future for this world and its children which you bear, and speak to the heart of the men you love so that they might see, and understand themselves, and so they might understand you. Lend them a hand, whilst showing patience and compassion, for they need to leave a world which is breaking, – and they do not know where to go. Now it is time to build new homes for them – new homes in your inner being, in your womb, so that they will build homes for you. There is nothing greater than a man and woman being unified in one spirit.

This was what I was striving for when I came. I did not know clearly then but I know it now. This is what I have dreamt about, what I have envisioned. Man and woman sharing – laughter, tenderness, values, intentions, plans, ... and children. To be each others body – in respect and trust. This was what I was looking for unceasingly in the men I have met, with the men I had love with – in one form or another.

I could not see it anymore in Charles – he and I – we had given up. It is sad. There was a possibility. There was a chance ... we did not use it ... too much had happened, too much worry, too much control, too much victimhood ... but there had been a chance, and even this chance and the months when we had been in true deep love – this was worth everything.

If it can be possible for the duration of a second, it can be possible for a whole lifetime. The future of this

Earth lies in a new type of relationship between men and women, because they always created the face and the fate of the world. If you look deep enough you will find that truth. If you want to find and be at peace with God, see it in the other person, see it in your children, and see God in everybody your meet. Acknowledge the spritit of God in everyone you hate, and all those who are sick and in trouble. Acknowledge the dignity and the integrity of God in those you would rather not touch. Overcome your fear of touching people, for it is your very skin which gives warmth and through which you can give of yourselves.

Give of yourself! Be courageous and give of yourself! Not with a sour face, but with a smile. If you have the resources, then dress beautifully. Make and keep your body beautiful. Do sports, dance, laugh, have fun, go into nature – and love your body. It is precious, so very precious. Love yourself. Love every moment you live. Love every breath you breathe.

You do not get rewards in heaven for worries and sorrow. You do not get medals for your noble retreats, for your hesitations, for your clinging to old securities or saving accounts. In heaven they have no pedestals for mumified sculptures of some sort of merit, or rewards for having kept etiquettes and protocols alive (to say „adead" would be better). This is not what is needed of you, or what is requested. This does not bring you into the Hall of Fame. There is no Hall of Fame, there is no such place and no rewards for martyrs in any name whatsoever. You are not spoken of as holy if you die in the name of...

This is all man made, and often very tragic.

Oct 4th, 1997

Enjoy your life. I enjoyed mine. Love, laugh, dance. When you dance and laugh many things are and become easier, and even the difficult things become a part of your dance. Then they can change, and get better. That is why I loved ballet so much – and I encourage all of you, who know and love me, to go on and give yourselves. Give the best of yourselves in ballet.

From here I see, that in many ways life is a dance. So, when you do your pirouettes and your pas de deux and your free dances you are close to life. Whenever I could dance – I was so much myself. I also liked sports – very much so. Swimming is also a kind of dance – a dance in the water – and you really can jump. Jumping is to experience freedom, but to dance, to whirl – it does not matter if it is a waltz, the Fox Trot, Samba, Rock'n roll or free – this is to move into the rhythms of life. It is very erotic. It touches all parts of your being. I loved to dance, most of the time Charles did not. So I danced with many others – and they were surprised. I gave myself to the dance. Therefore they had all kinds of strange ideas.

A partner dance, yes it is close. If you dance, you cannot stay bitter. If you really give yourself when dancing, you can neither stay bitter towards yourself, nor towards your dance partner or even to the fellow dancers in the room. Is that the reason most people do not want to dance?

I invented many kinds of dances, which those who knew me, know. It was my kind of dance – I was close, I was intimate. Because it is more than just moving. It is moving TOGETHER. It does not matter if you touch the other person or not. You move together, you have eye contact – you look at one another, you see eachother, you discover eachother, you enjoy eachother. Dancing could heal many broken marriages and partnerships.

It is such a pity! Most of them do not dare to go beyond the resistance – it is like that everywhere – you need to forgive your partner when you dance – otherwise your body stays stiff. Do you understand? You have to want to go beyond the pride and the bitterness you are holding, as these are the things that are making you stiff, lifeless and sick.

How much money I have made by dancing (she laughs) – and so can you. Dancing brings wealth and richness to your life. That is not necessarily money, but it makes your life richer and it throws out all old behaviour, and all this stuckness. If you dance and laugh, laugh. If you dance and cry, cry – but dance. Often when I was so desperate in Kensington or somewhere – at times when I was alone, I played music, and I danced for myself – a kind of aerobic dance, yes, but it was a dance – and I let my laughter, my crying, my agonies, and my despairs go.

I was not a martyr, and I am not one. Please do not make me one. Sometimes I might have acted like one, and it may have looked like the behaviour of a martyr. There were papers who said I looked like the Madonna in Pain. Yes, it is true – I know the Giotto picture and others – I often looked at those and I saw myself in them, the Queen of Heaven, the mother in pain.

I have born two sons, and they are no martyrs – when you saw them walking behind my coffin – did you see martyrs? I did not. I was very proud of them.

I do not want them to become idols either. It is not a good place to be. An idol is always in danger of being pushed off the pedestal. An idol is never really understood, or seen in the essence. It is always the subject of projections of one sort or the other.

The zig-zag of my ways had something good, I hope. Perhaps it was that I was slipping out from under the cover of an idol. I wanted to be and to stay Diana – not even Princess of Wales, not even Lady Di, nor the future queen – just Diana, maybe Miss, mummy, Di.

I was not an idol, and I do not want to become one. That is why I wanted to talk here. I wanted to offer you a Diana you can think of, you can be with – as a friend, as a companion – maybe as a teacher, which is what I wanted to be and become so much in a phase of my life, a teacher, who would convey knowledge in a tender loving way.

I was not a martyr – but pain I knew, yes, the pain of deepest helplessness. The pain of not being able to find either any way out, or any way in – into the heart of people, into the heart of a man.

Finally I found the way into the heart of a man – and it led to a way out.

Today, the day that what I am saying here is being written down, "today" (what a strange word) is the day of Francis of Assisi. How much I loved the stories of this man. He talked with animals, and he knew their soul.

I talked with animals too, I even talked with trees, and often hugged one, or embraced a flower. They had all names. I talked with my dogs, I talked with my pony, the geese, the rabbits, the cats – and they all had their own character. Whenever we could manage to visit a Zoo I taught my sons and also the children in the kindergarden to see animals as beings with souls, who are sensitive, each of them having a special character. They feel pain and joy as we do. Their instinctiveness, and their natural trust in us humans are a challenge for us. If they could really defend themselves, the premises would be different, but they cannot. They are in our hands, and we are responsible.

You may and can do with animals whatever you want – outwardly, but they belong to the Earth which cannot be controlled. The cries of tortured animals fill the cosmos. What I have seen and also went against in my lifetime and still do now, is that you use animals in your world to satisfy a pretty morbid lust, namely the lust to show power to somebody who is already in your power – just for the "fun" of it. It does not matter if the fun is, to make more money, to breed new species who are in torture for a lifetime, to stick your fingers into DNA technology or something else. It is the morbid lust to misuse power – where the true power would be care, that is CARE for those who are in your power.

You know, the Spencers and the Windsors have enjoyed hunting for generations. I never was keen on that. I never liked it ... but hunting, true hunting, does give more chance to an animal than to breed them in prison and kill them slowly through a lifetime of suffering. Most animals who are carried to the slaughterhouses are already dead. One is eating "double-dead" meat. Smell this meat. It has the smell of death, of decay. It it not really digestable. It goes into ones body and stays there harming it... letting one decay.

I was not so conscious about that during my lifetime, – but my bulimia was partly influenced by my thoughts about meat and its origin.

Life is vulnerable. All life is connected. Each of you is connected to the soul of each animal in your world. Everything you do to an animal you do to yourselves. Just once, only one time did I hurt an animal in my lifetime, and the repercussions I felt hurt me very deeply, so I was off for days. Also on one occasion an animal hurt me, or at least I thought so. After that I was off for days and weeks. (I forgive you, please forgive me).

You, reader, are as sensitive as I am, in the essence, because I was not more a human being than you are – so whatever you do with animals – indirectly or directly – you do with yourself. Think about it. It is absolute truth, and Saint Francis of Assisi knew it.

There are people in your world who speak with animals. There are those who care dearly for them. There are those who strive for these brothers and sisters of mankind. Support them, as much you support those who care for their fellow humans.

Support the organizations I have patronized. Help them to stay and maintain their work. Let them build networks. I can see thousands of them – it does not matter if they are founded in my name or not. My name stands for something – so it could help, if they are founded or associated with my name.

Go on William, keep them up, care for them and found new ones – and you Harry, support your brother! Be a team! You know, what I mean.

Oslo. I am very glad about the conference and its results. But this cannot stop here – it is only a beginning. You need to find a way to make it known. There are those who are already thinking about how they can replace the landmines with something even more atrocious, and more hidious. Others even laugh about the contracts – so you need to find proper ways to check. You need to go into the interiors of your countries to look and see where they produce that kind of stuff.

Also many of you are hypocrites. You still support the production of all kinds of terrible weapons (to defend what – my goodness, what do you want do defend ...? Life ...?) and you are saying that it is in order to maintain jobs, to maintain economy. Can you see the total craziness of this kind of thinking? If there is a bomb exploding – somewhere in the world – it kills the very man, who did not want to lose his job in a weapon factory?!

How much I loved Sadat – him and Egypt, the new Egypt is like the new England – it can bring peace and freedom. I do not say it out of an old traditional patriotism, or to undermine the spirit of Europe, and neither do I say it out of my love to Dodi, nor do I support any form of ideology or fundamentalism – I say it, because of the social, political, cutural and spiritual potentials these two countries have.

Mubarak and his counsellors! Remember Sadat, remember the legacy of his life. Egypt has a magic from long ago – as England has. England has so many healers and givers, so many, who know how to use their personal power, their creativity, their visions correctly and with Integrity.

Egypt has an old promise. It is the golden land – no, not the only one, but a very special one. It has the potential of an alchemy to bring those brothers together – the Islamic and the Judaeic worlds as they were united once before. It is necessary and important, this synergy is on the brink of leading either into total destruction or total peace and renewal. It is part of the birth ... part of the decision, where the world will go.

That is why the powers of old, the powers of schism and fundamentalism want to hinder it – but it is not possible to resist in the long run. Egypt has this magic power in each ounce of its soil – so see what will happen. The two spirits which are together here are going together there and finding the synergy. This is one of the reasons of our death, and nothing can be done – nothing can be stopped. It only can lead into one of both directions. The choice is yours.

I do not want to be misunderstood. I love all people and all religions. I always have. I love Hindus and Buddhists, Jews and Palestinians – because all are people. If you would just understand that you are all people. The physical forms you obtain and defend, while you are in the world, lose every meaning even their existence when one arrives here. All those who sacrifice their lives in the name of whatever, they come here and think: "What in all the world did I do and think ... none of it is true...the only truth is that I have hurt others ... that I did not let my heart speak but only my mind, my ego, my ideology". And for these souls this is very painful ... and only the love and the light of friends and helpers can bring healing and hope to such a soul ... a soul which is crushed into the deepest despair about itself ... think about this ... the forms fall away .. the essence is seen ... and the essence is the love of the heart and the compassion you performed... nothing else matters or ever has mattered.

Again there is no Hall of Fame, not in the name of any religion. Believe me, those, who in their fanatism killed themselves and many others, come here in deep despair, not knowing how to give peace to their souls and many must help them, so that they can see and be healed. Know that the light, the love and the truth in this place here allow you to look VERY differently at your life – you see your life with no spectacles whatsoever, you see yourself naked, as a former human being, as a soul – completely equal to any other soul. Here are no "better thans" or "less thans".

Here, the very souls who hurt each other are falling into each others arms, crying, asking for forgiveness. In the place you call heaven, which is VERY real, in some ways more real than the world you come from, there ARE NO RELIGIONS. There are only souls – only. It is they who see and evaluate what they have done. There is no hell, and no purgatory, but just a clear look, maybe a very painful look, but a clear look. If death, the knowing that you will die, if this could be a teacher for you, that you go through a stage, when you realize who you really are, and that you are received in love and truth – you would live even more powerful and peaceful lives.

None of the founders of any religion WANTED what is happening in their names on Earth. Even for those who come here and have been admired on Earth as heroes, there is no heroism here. The titles, the rules and regulations, the etiquettes and protocols, the medals, prices and rewards – they are not of interest.

What is of interest is what you have learned and how much you have succeeded in being authentic, being yourself, human. How much you have lived in peace with your soul, and given her space to express herself. How much you have given of the wealth of your heart, talents and skills, and the riches you blindly accumulate and become so easiliy stuck with. What also counts is how much (clean) fun you had, and how much clean fun and pleasure you gave to others. How much of your integrity combined with the truth of your heart and the compassion of your mind you have shared – beyond state and race, religion and borders. These are the things which echoe here.

Life is considered a play – yes. It is a play and it is a significant play. It is a play of creation – where you create what is true and valuable for yourself, thus adding to the truth and value of life, no matter how often you come.

I have come often – and many times I was connected to royalty or played a role there. It is not hard to find this out – and it is not important. Next time I might come as a teacher – because I like to teach. Although I did not become queen in my lifetime, I have become one now.

Some papers say, that I was supposed to be the "ticket" into the 21th century. Dear ones, ticket for whom and what? You are all your own ticket. You can read this and wonder. You can be angry with the man, who wrote this and you can be angry with those, who distributed it. You can deny my spirit in this, or you can look for the essence of me in what is written here.

I can say things here, which I could not in my lifetime. One reason is – I was too young. Being young and pretty had its purpose. The times needed it ... and it fulfilled a very personal purpose.

You can either look for all the doubts and the "mistakes" in these lines, or you can look for a testimony which confirms the testimony in your own heart. I am not the ticket into the new century. But clearly, I am a lead, a hint, a clue for what it is necessary to be in order to make your new century beautiful, wondrous, successful and worth living in. Many, many changes will come. Many changes will be necessary. Many will try to resist them. Some will even try to pull all elements, all weapons, money and "subjects" together to prohibit the new – the new that is to come, and will come.

See, pregnancy and birth teach us something. After nine month, more or less, the baby has developed enough to need to be born. One can yammer, one can resist it, but the pain will become even stronger. It WILL be born. The child of the New Age WILL be born – and no might, no power can resist it. Just as you cannot resist the sun rising and setting, or the rain dropping onto your housetop, neither can this be stopped – whatever you do. The new, the change is coming – and the change comes out of the heart of people. It always was and always will be. It is stronger than anything that exists because everything that exists is from the heart – fundamentally. This heart is longsuffering – but it will renew itsef as in a birth, like a little bird, and it will break the egg shells, because it wants to live, as tender as it is ... and as weak as it appears.

This was my message and my mission: to prepare a way for this birth, to prepare a way and a strength in your heart so you can more easily let this birth happen.

The Berlin Walls came down because of the hearts of people – politicians worked on it for tens of years. The hearts of the people will change the monarchy and the ways of the government of England, Scottland, and Ireland – and I have my reasons why I mention them separately. The strength of Great Britain (if it wants to stay together) is their synergy and their visions. The monarchy with Charles and with William is, can, and must be the spirit, who helps Blair, those to come, and all people, to build the new Britain – whatever form it will have. Charles should trust his new relationship to the men, women and children of Britain, with his new and fresh thoughts and ideas regarding the monarchy and its functions. He can prepare the way for William, and the people of Britain will love him. When the time is ripe – and it will be seen clearly – William will be king and I will be with him.

I thank all of you who contributed to my life. Many I did not mention by name – my friends, relatives, sisters – all those who made my work and my life a place of success or a place of learning or both. Each one of you – the way you have been, was perfect.

It is my will, that nobody who participated in my life or death should be investigated, taken to court or harmed in any way. This would obscure my mission and my purpose – and there are some who would like to do that. Leave their families and relatives and associates unharmed – let them have their peace. Nobody, nobody is guilty – because I have chosen the course of my life exactly the way it was. This is the main message of the book you read here.

In my lifetime I sometimes had the feeling of revenge, or even of deep rage, I blamed, and I made others guilty ... but I think I often showed you that I was ready to overcome these feelings. Furthermore, in the blissful and happy state that I have now, I do not hold any grudges against anybody. I can see the picture clearly. It is like a carpet of many patterns, or a pattern of waves in an endless ocean. I decided to live and die in the way I did – and all of you do too.

So forgive me for when I have harmed you, worried you or gave you reasons for bewilderment or frustration. I have been a human being – so are you. Life is learning – and dear Marilyn, yes „nobody is perfect“.

All of you I did not mention here be clear that I love you. I love you from the depth of my heart and I will always love you.

With this love I thank you, author of this book and all of you, who contribute to it being published and distributed. You are under my personal protection.

All the happiness, joy and fulfillment to you – Christina and Inaki on this day, the day of your wedding.

I will go and complete my course of lives, and so will you. Keep up the good works and speak good of each other.

Farewell, good bye and ... see you again.
God bless you.

In my deepest love ...

Diana

A word from the author

Dear reader,

in the week following the terrible death of Lady Di, a very important person in my personal life died, an event which moved me deeply.

I sat at my father's bedside, and was able to be with him at the time of his death. I will never forget the grace and the peace that filled my parents' house. I experienced being very close to death – perhaps better expressed as "close to that other world", the living world beyond death.

The next day, still under the influence of these events, I went into my office, and started to write an obituary for my father. What happened next was extraordinary. A voice began to introduce itself, at first indistinct, but all the time becoming clearer. I knew this voice. I put the obituary aside, and started writing, the first page, that is the first page of this book, on 5th September 1997. While I was writing, I felt a very strong and loving energy, that was filled with light, flooding the room.

I sent a fax to my publisher, Christa Falk, and briefly described my experiences to her.

In the course of the following week this energy and light became stronger. On 7th September I wrote some more pages, but then I decided to stop all this, because I did not know what to do with it all, and I had so many other "more important" things to get on with..

A few days later when Mrs. Falk telephoned me, it became clear during our conversation that something of great value was taking place. It was apparent that Diana still had some things, that she would have liked to have expressed in her lifetime, to tell her relatives, everybody whom she loved, and the world.

The thing that was particularly important to her was this, that no one should be damaged in any way by her death, that nobody be declared guilty, called to account, or persuaded to give evidence, and that no disputes should arise from it. None of that was important any more. In fact it would be detrimental, as it would cast a dark shadow over the memory of her, the things she has said and has to say, and the purpose of her life. Also it would be very hard for her, if, by the means of her death, she had caused those reactions. Therefore she implores us to refrain from all such things. I understand this very well, and this was partly why I wanted to fulfil her wishes.

So on 23rd September, 25th September and from 1st October to 4th October 1997, I carried on writing.The 3rd and 4th of October were days when the energy was particularly strong again. In this book I have passed on exactly what she said to me on those days, so this is the only version of it.

Finally I had a book in front of me which had touched me very deeply as I was receiving it.

It is my hope that you will be moved and encouraged by these pages, and that Diana will speak to your heart, just as she spoke to mine – with all of this incredible love that came from the "Queen of Hearts", and still is coming from her.

Dietrich von Oppeln

The German edition of this title is

Diana

Ich möchte euch so gerne noch etwas sagen ...

ISBN 3-89568-044-3

ch. falk-verlag